THE VILLAGE CHURCH

BOTTISFORD CHURCH, LINCOLNSHIRE

THE VILLAGE CHURCH

BY

P. H. DITCHFIELD

M.A., F.S.A., F.R.S.L., F.R.Hist.S.

WITH 15 ILLUSTRATIONS

EP PUBLISHING LIMITED
1975

First published 1914 by Methuen & Co. Ltd.

Republished 1975 by
EP Publishing Limited
East Ardsley, Wakefield
West Yorkshire, England

by kind permission of the copyright holders
Copyright © 1975 Methuen & Co. Ltd.

ISBN 0 7158 1131 2

Please address all enquiries to EP Publishing Limited
(address as above)

Printed in Great Britain by
The Scolar Press, Limited,
Ilkley, West Yorkshire

PREFACE

DURING the last thirty years it has been the privilege of the writer to visit village churches in various parts of England, and especially in Berkshire and the neighbouring counties. He has made notes on their architectural features and contents, and this book is the result of his antiquarian wanderings. The large and increasing number of those who take a keen interest in our ecclesiastical buildings of the smaller type may find it useful in helping them to understand the origin, meaning, and signification of that which they discover in the churches which they visit, and to know what to look for.

A typical village church has been chosen for illustration, and each part examined—walls, buttress, tower, parapet, porch, nave, chancel, and chantry, as well as its interior fittings and adornments. Particular examples are given of the details of churches, and certain chapters describe the fonts, mural paintings, wood-carvings, and other furniture and ornaments with which the skill and piety of former generations of church-folk have enriched the Houses of God throughout our land. It is hoped that this method of treatment may stimulate interest in our churches and attract the general reader more than any dry and learned treatise on architectural styles that appeals mainly to the expert.

I have tried to avoid, as far as possible, difficult architectural terms, and when I have been obliged to use them I have in most instances explained their meaning. It has not, therefore, been deemed necessary to supply a glossary of architectural words. If one should be found needful the reader is referred to T. D. Atkinson's *Glossary of Terms used in English Architecture* (Methuen & Co., 3s. 6d. net), or to the writer's former book, *Handbook of Gothic Architecture*, published at a small cost by Messrs. Dent & Sons, wherein I have given a list of architectural terms with sketches of each object.

I beg to acknowledge much assistance that I have derived from the works of architectural experts and from other workers in the field of ecclesiastical archaeology. Especially am I grateful to my friend Mr. Charles E. Keyser, F.S.A., in whose company I have explored many a village church, and from whose descriptions I have derived much profit. Mr. Keyser's books on

Norman Doorways and *Mural Paintings* are invaluable. The works of another friend of the author, the Rev. Dr. J. Charles Cox, have been most useful, especially the admirable series, *The Antiquary's Books*, of which he is the general editor, and also his series of *County Churches*. Of the former, the volumes on *English Church Furniture,* edited by himself and Dr. Harvey, *The Brasses of England,* by the Rev. H. W. Macklin, Canon Raven's *Bells of England,* and Mr. Philip Nelson's *Ancient Painted Glass in England,* have frequently been consulted, and some of the illustrations that appear in this book have been selected from them by the publishers, Messrs. Methuen & Co., who are also the publishers of the *Antiquary's Books.*

The works of an elder generation of writers on ecclesiological subjects have also supplied much valuable information—Francis Dollman's *Ancient Pulpits,* Paley's *Illustrations of Baptismal Fonts,* and others—and amongst modern books I beg to acknowledge the assistance of two admirably written works published by Messrs. Wells Gardner, Darton & Co. ; *Towers and Spires,* by Mr. E. Tyrrell Green ; and *Porches and Fonts,* by Mr. J. Charles Wall. Mr. Francis Bond's numerous works, especially on *Wood-Carvings in English Churches,* have been studied, and many other books consulted. I am grateful to Mr. Keyser for his kind permission to reproduce a photograph of the

Norman doorway at Lullington, and also one of the windows of his church at Aldermaston, which appeared in his article on that church in the *Berks, Bucks, and Oxon Archaeological Journal*. My thanks are also due for useful information derived from the books of Mr. A. Hamilton Thompson, F.S.A., and for that which has been supplied by several friends and correspondents.

P. H. DITCHFIELD

BARKHAM RECTORY
September, 1914

CONTENTS

LIST OF ILLUSTRATIONS

THE VILLAGE CHURCH

THE VILLAGE CHURCH

CHAPTER I

INTRODUCTION

IN almost every English village there stands a fine old church which tells the story, writ in stone, of centuries of parochial and religious life, and which is remarkable for its picturesqueness, its architectural beauties, and its interesting associations. It has been since its foundation, dating back to the dawn of Christianity in England, the centre of the activities of the villagers, both religious, secular, and social. Its vestry has been the council-chamber of the parish, wherein the village managed its own concerns ; within its walls the voices of praise and worship, of instruction and exhortation have been raised century after century. It is intimately connected with the chief events in the lives of each generation of the inhabitants of the hamlet. To its font the infant, " puling in its nurse's arms," was brought for baptism. As he grew older within its walls he learned the mysteries of the Faith, and as time went on one day he led his bride to the altar and they became man and wife. Time passes ; he sees his sons and daughters grow up and marry. A wrinkled old man, crippled with rheumatism, he hobbles to church, and ere long he is brought there for the last time, and a gravestone marks his memory. Such is the story of each human life the church tells. Squire and peasant, priest and knight and lord lie there, great statesman and humble rustic. We read the histories in brass memorials or ponderous monuments of the men who have wrought great deeds for Church or country and the rude rhymes that are inscribed on many a tombstone in God's acre telling of the affectionate regard of those who reared it for dear ones mourned.

The old grey church, set in its framework of high elms, with its yew-tree near its entrance, is the greatest charm of the village. Its architectural story tells of the builders of former days, of their striving after improvements and higher flights of achievement, how in each century they sought to make their House of God more worthy of Him whom within its walls they worshipped. We can trace their working and notice how, wearied by the dull massiveness of the Romanesque style of the twelfth century, they strove to make the masonry lighter and inserted their lancet windows and raised their pointed arches. Some squire in the fourteenth century added a chantry chapel wherein he provided the services of a priest to pray for the souls of himself and his family, and the windows have graceful tracery and exhibit the highest art of English architectural achievement. The village prospered and the inhabitants increased ; so in the next century they added a south aisle, and imagining that that style then prevalent in England was far superior to anything that had been done before (an illusion that was not confined to the fifteenth century), destroyed some of the earlier work and substituted new arcades and large Perpendicular windows and much else that the new architectural fashion dictated. Later on the Renaissance builders erected a new porch, and then, perhaps, the western tower showed signs of decay and was considered dangerous ; so the inhabitants decided to raise money to build a fine new brick tower for their bells, which they loved to ring on all occasions and had been debarred from doing so by the shakiness of the old structure. In this manner the church grew, and proclaims by its stones its story and the good work of the English masons who wrought simply, naturally, unaffectedly, in their own native way, using the materials Nature provided for them. It reflects, too, the charity and religious feelings of the people, who often, unaided by lord or abbot, with their own hands effected all these alterations and improvements for the honour and glory of the Most High and for the well-being of the village.

Our churches have suffered sadly from mutilation, desecration, and over-restoration ; but in spite of all the changes wrought by time and circumstances it is possible in many churches to trace the modes in which our fathers worshipped, the position of the several altars, the Easter sepulchre and its uses, the ancient ritual, the consecration crosses, the misericords in the chancel, the position of the rood-screen, the squints or hagioscopes, the parvise and chantry. It is possible still to admire the productions of ancient art that time and vandalism have spared, the mural paintings, the old stained glass, the carvings and sculpture, the encaustic tiles and painted screens, the beautifully carved bench-ends or the Jacobean pulpit, and much else that may be discovered in village churches.

We do not intend to extend our travels in order to visit important town churches, with their larger structures and more complete arrangements. Our quest is the church of the village, the old building that has looked down with a fostering care upon the rural hamlet through all the centuries and been regarded by its people as their home, their spiritual house, that has been associated with all the joys and sorrows of their earthly pilgrimage, its voice plainly uttered by the spire rising above the trees, ever whispering to their hearts, *Sursum corda!* Its bells have tolled out many a knell for friend and dear one ; its joyous peal has found an echo in many a heart, and as year by year the mourners deck with flowers the graves of those they have " lost awhile " they feel a sense of the sweet communion which living men and women enjoy with those whose work is done and of the building of that " spiritual house not made with hands, eternal in the heavens."

We shall penetrate the vestry, and there perhaps find time to open the old iron safe, examine the registers—" the short and simple annals of the poor "—the Church plate, the church-wardens' account-books, which reveal how the work of the parish was carried on before the days of the Poor Law Unions and the abolition of Church Rates and the formation of Highway Boards, and much else that enlarges the rates which poor parsons and farmers have to pay and makes them sigh for the " good old days " when those who paid the money had a voice in the spending of it, and could spend it on their own village and in support of their own people, and were not obliged to send it to some central authority to pay the salaries of a host of officials. The churchwardens used to conduct the affairs of the parish without emolument or fee ; and if sometimes they did have a meal or some refreshment at the expense of the rates, they had earned it admirably by their gratuitous labours.

Imagine you see a typical village church. It stands not far removed from the centre of the village.   It is probably built on a site that was regarded with religious awe long before Christianity came to our shores.   There are several instances in which churches have been built on British or Saxon barrows or tumuli, wherein the dead bodies of the primitive inhabitants of Britain were interred.   In East Yorkshire there is at least one instance.   British bodies lie beneath the church of Fimber in a tumulus composed of clay obtained from a neighbouring local deposit, and a skeleton was found therein with some pottery, flint instruments, and animal bones.   The oratory of Chapel Carn Brea, in Cornwall, surmounts a tumulus.   At Taplow, Bucks, there is a tumulus in the churchyard which contained the body of a Saxon chieftain, with jewels and other objects, now in the British Museum.   A cromlech, locally known as the giant's grave, is in the churchyard at Penrith.   Doubtless many other instances could be quoted to show that the site of the present church has been set apart for some religious purpose from very early times, before the advent of the Christian missionaries.   Divers paths lead to it, called church walks, pleasant avenues along which there has been a right of way from time immemorial.   It is the birthright of every Englishman to be able to get to his parish church ; hence these walks were made high and dry above the low meadows and kept in repair by the churchwardens out of the Church Rates.

Shakespeare alluded to them when he wrote, " The why is plain as way to parish church." We shall notice the various styles of architecture exemplified in the building, the materials of its construction, the lych-gate, the porch, the doorways, windows, buttresses, the curious carvings of strange beasts that adorn its exterior, the tower, nave, chancel, font, and each part of the structure that delights our eyes and makes us long to know its use and cause and origin. We shall examine its peculiar features—and each church seems to possess some peculiarities. They differ in size, structure and material, and in appearance quite as much as men's faces differ. You can seldom see two exactly alike. But we shall try to understand the peculiar features of our typical church, and this may enable us to interpret aright the meaning of the structures of other ecclesiastical buildings.

We are writing, not for the architectural expert who understands all mysteries and all knowledge, but for the ordinary reader who loves to visit our old village churches, takes an intelligent interest in their story, admires their beauties, and wishes to know more of the origin and meaning of the things that he sees. The motorist rushes through our villages, sometimes takes a hasty glance at the church, and hurries on his way. If he would condescend to stay a little longer and to suffer us to point out to him the hidden secrets of the building, perhaps he would enjoy his tour much more, and store his mind with the memories of objects which only require a little mental effort in order to be appreciated. May we hope, too, that this book may be of some service to the villagers themselves, enabling them to realize what treasures they have stored in the church they love, and to take an intelligent interest in the wealth of antiquity and history that a study of their own parish church affords.

CHAPTER II

THE PLAN AND SHAPE OF THE CHURCH

OUR typical village church, that looks so fair among the trees, was originally cruciform, consisting of a nave, a chancel with central tower, and north and south transepts were added later. We like to think that this plan was devised in order to represent the sacred emblem of Christianity, the Holy Cross on which the Saviour died, just as we would wish to interpret the inclining of the plan of the chancel to the north or south as signifying the leaning of the head of the Saviour when He died after the Crucifixion. But such interpretations are fanciful and are not to be relied upon. The story of the development of the plan of an English church is a long one, and can only be briefly sketched here.

The earliest plan of a British church is shown in that which was unearthed at Silchester, in Hampshire, the well-known Roman city, which was thoroughly excavated and examined by the Society of Antiquaries.[1]   Our churches are almost all

---

[1] The foundations of this church have been entirely covered up, but a very accurate model may be seen in the Reading Museum.

orientated, the chancel and altar being placed at the east end. In this Silchester church, as in some others at Rome and elsewhere, the sanctuary was at the west end, and the priest standing at the west of the altar faced the east when he celebrated Holy Communion. A little square of tesselated pavement marked the site of the altar. This church was based on the model of the Roman basilica or court of justice or exchange. There was an atrium or open forecourt, with a well or fountain in the centre. There was a nave with aisles and a narthax or porch covering the whole of the eastern front, and on the west an apse with two pseudo-transepts on each side of it, separated by walls from the aisles and so forming chambers. In this respect and with regard to the narthax this little church shows Eastern rather than Roman influence, and exemplifies the connection of the Celtic Church with that of Gaul and with the early missionaries who came from Asia and converted Southern Gaul to the Christian faith.

But all Celtic or Romano-British churches were not so elaborate, and many consisted of a plain oblong with an altar at one end. To this was added a chancel for the celebration of the holy mysteries.

The plans of other churches constructed in Saxon times show an aisleless nave with a square-ended chancel divided from it by a solid wall pierced by a narrow arch, and one or more porches on the north or south side of large size. Such are the very interesting churches of Bradford-on-Avon in Wiltshire and Escomb, while in Kent there are evidences of the existence of churches with an aisleless nave, eastern apse, a western porch, and chapels on the north and south, which produce a cruciform plan. The fact that these were added later shows that there was no intention originally of making the plan in the shape of a cross. Much activity in church-building was evident in the north under the leadership of Benedict Biscop and St. Wilfrid in the seventh century, and these churches conformed in plan with the Gaulish basilicas. It is well known that St. Wilfrid always strove to reform the customs and usages of Celtic Christianity, and, as the Council of Whitby proves, to conform them to the Roman use. These northern churches, the plans of which can still be traced, are Monkwearmouth, Jarrow, and Hexham. There is another important Saxon church at Brixworth, built in the last half of the seventh century, which has for its plan an oblong chancel with apse, a nave with aisles, and at the west end a porch, on the north and south of which are doorways. At Wing, in Buckinghamshire, there is a polygonal apse.

Such are some of the more elaborately planned churches of the early Saxon period ; but the ordinary plan was an aisleless nave and chancel, with sometimes a porch at the west end and chapels jutting out on the sides of the nave. Later on, instead of the western porch, the builders erected a tower, and then, as at Barton-on-Humber, a rectangular structure west of this tower ; and the tower, enlarged to the width of the nave, became the actual nave of the church, a chancel being added on the east side. North and south of the tower chapels were built, which afterwards developed into transepts. Thus the tower became the central part of the building, and we have not far to go to develop the cruciformed building of Norman times.

When the great era of Norman building set in after the Conquest, the masons set to work to improve the old Saxon churches. They rebuilt them, sometimes preserving the aisleless plan, but more often constructing aisles, taking down the Saxon walls and erecting arcades, and building their massive piers and walls. The story of the apse would take a long time to tell. It was never a favourite form in England, and although the Norman builders, especially the monkish masons, were partial to it, it never found favour, and frequently the English reverted to the square end. Mr. S. Hamilton Thompson [1] suggests that it was lack of skill on the part of local builders in planning and stone-cutting that caused this hesitancy to adopt new fashions ; but it is also evident that in many cases apses were removed

[1] *The Ground Plan of the English Parish Church*, p. 50.

and, in accordance with native sentiment, the square end substituted. We have in some village churches traced apses on the east side of transepts, but these have in most cases disappeared, though their foundations remain under the turf of the churchyard.

We notice the same clinging to the native style in the treatment of the porch. Saxon porches were large and roomy, as at Bradford-on-Avon. The Norman builders introduced a very shallow and insignificant porch, but the native art triumphed in the end, and in the thirteenth century the porch again became a dignified and important structure.

We have traced the course of the planning, the formation of the central tower, which in Saxon times did not rest on piers and arches, but was a solid structure with narrow doors opening into chancel, nave, and side chapels. The Norman masons, more confident in their skill, erected their centred towers on massive piers, and produced a unity of design in the building. In the thirteenth and fourteenth centuries, in order to meet the requirements of increased ritual, the small chancels were often pulled down and rebuilt on a larger scale. Collegiate churches or priories attached to some monastery were often founded in villages, and the chancels were used by the canons or monks, and enlarged and fitted with carved oaken stalls with misericords. In larger churches the increased veneration of the Blessed Virgin caused the erection of a Lady Chapel. A chantry was added by some great landowner, who founded it in order that Masses might be sung for the repose of his soul and those of his relations and friends. In the fifteenth century the plans of churches were somewhat changed. The chancel ceased to be a secluded sanctuary, and a large aisleless nave, as at Winchcombe, in Gloucestershire, built by the last Abbot, became the favourite plan.

Such, in very brief, is the story of the planning of our churches. We see how it developed from age to age, until at last the church assumed the shape and form it bears to-day.

It is necessary to study the process of its formation before passing on to the description of the details of our village church. The story may seem dull and uninteresting to the reader, but it is instructive and obligatory if he would attempt to understand the significance of the various parts of the building. He may, if he will, expand it by carefully studying and drawing the ground plans of the various churches he visits, comparing one with another, and thus forming a true conception of the infinite variety of our churches and of the skill of the English masons who devised them.

CHAPTER III

THE EXTERIOR

WE will, first, walk round the church and admire its external beauties and general details. The walling sometimes proclaims the age of the original building. At the corners of the tower we can detect some " long and short work "—*i.e.*, a stone of some length, set up perpendicularly, alternating with a shorter stone set horizontally. This is usually considered a sign of the Saxon mason's art. Herring-bone work, consisting of a layer of stones laid slantways in one direction, while above this row is another line of stones leaning the opposite way, is also an indication of early work, though this mode of building was also occasionally used by Norman masons. Saxon walling is rude and rough, having large blocks of stones set in thick layers of mortar. Of windows and doors we shall write at length later on. And here we may indicate the various styles of architecture that prevailed during the Gothic period.

    1. Anglo-Saxon style existed until about the end of the eleventh century.

2. Norman style prevailed during the twelfth century.
3. From 1175 to 1200 there was a period of transition from the massive Norman to the Early English style.
4. Early English, 1200-1275.
5. Transitional, 1275-1300.
6. Decorated, 1300-1375.
7. Transitional, 1375-1400.
8. Perpendicular, 1400-1500.
9. Tudor, 1500-1558.
10. Early Renaissance, 1558-1625.
11. Later Renaissance, 1625-1714.
12. Georgian style, 1714-1800.

These dates are only approximate. Changes of style did not always take place at one and the same time in all parts of the country, as though some secret and mystic movement had made its way through the shires and stirred the hearts and nerved the hands of all the masons and artificers throughout England. Some shires were quick to catch the new architectural inspiration ; others worked on in their old modes and were slowly influenced by new ideas and ideals. But it is remarkable how soon they spread in spite of the isolation of country villages before the days of stage-coaches, railways, or motor-cars, and in spite of the conservative nature of the English character.

Leaving doors and windows until a later chapter, we will continue our walk round the church, and before us stands a buttress supporting the wall. This has a story to tell. The walls of Norman buildings were strong and massive, could well withstand the thrust of the roof, and needed little external support. Hence buttresses were built almost flush with the wall, only slightly projecting. But in the thirteenth century the masons were striving after " sweetness and light." They made their walls less heavy and their buildings higher and more graceful. Hence the thrust on the walls was greater, and the buttress was made to project farther from the wall. This was found so effective that the masons discovered that it was not necessary to make them so wide. They projected much more at the foot than at the summit, and receded by one or more stages, each stage being marked by a " set-off." In the fourteenth century the buttress received more elaborate treatment. In the front space was found for a niche for an image, and this niche has a finely carved crocketed canopy, and above this a little gable, and there are on each side crocketed finials, and the buttress has developed into a finely ornamented piece of work, very different from the flat, rectangular mass of masonry designed by the Norman builders to support the wall.

A little farther on we come to another buttress, very similar to the last in shape and size, but carved panelling is seen upon its surface. This is the hall-mark of Perpendicular work, and shows that it was erected in the fifteenth century or in Tudor days. The upper stages differ from the lower ones, and are often octagonal or hexagonal, and each side has canopies at the top, and a great crocketed pinnacle crowns the buttress. Our ideal church has a clerestory, rising clear above the aisles, and upon this the roof rests. Hence the pressure of this roof, especially if it was vaulted, was a heavy burden upon the walls of the clerestory, which could not be supported by buttresses. How was this difficulty to be overcome? The outer walls of the aisles had their support given by buttresses, but how were these clerestory walls to be held up and sustained? Our masonic ancestors were ingenious folk. They had these external buttresses. Why not bridge over the space between these and the walls of the clerestory by an arch which, with one foot resting on the buttress, would hold up the wall and enable it to sustain the roof? And thus there came into being the flying buttress, which is an amazing thing of beauty as well as a powerful prop for holding up the fabric. In some of our large churches and cathedrals, and in such magnificent buildings as that at Amiens, we see the extraordinary development of this prominent and beautiful feature of mediæval architecture. In our village churches we sometimes see useful and charming examples of flying buttresses.

Jutting out from the roof are strange and weird

grotesque animals or figures carved in stone, which form projecting waterspouts, and are called gurgoyles. They were not always confined to churches, as the following ancient verse testifies :—

> And every house covered was with lead,
> And many a gurgoyle and many a hideous head
> And spouts through, and pipes as they ought
> From the stonework to the kennel brought.

But these curious forms and spouts were chiefly used in the building of churches, and there are some good reasons why they were placed there. The old churches built by the Normans have none of these fantastic creatures, and it was not until the thirteenth century dawned that these strange images began to show themselves in England. The period of Early English architecture gave birth to them, and each succeeding period continued their existence. There they are still, and as we go to church the grinning countenances of hideous monsters—dragons, demons, fabulous animals, and extraordinary human beings—look down upon us and seem to scoff at us.

What was the object of the builders and architects in placing such strange creatures on a sacred building? They were not always approved of by the great ecclesiastics who lived at the time they were carved. For instance, St. Bernard wrote in the year 1125 to William, Abbot of St. Thierry, to this effect : " To what good are all these grotesque monsters in painting and sculpture? What are the significations of these foul monkeys, these furious lions, and these monstrous centaurs? What are the meanings attached to these warriors and the hunters who are blowing horns, or these quadrupeds with serpents' tails?"

But in spite of St. Bernard all these grotesque figures have some meaning. Some think that these sculptures of the hideous objects on the outside of religious buildings are the emblems of human vices, and are placed there to warn those who enter God's house that they must leave outside all the evil passions which soil the soul and make them unfit to worship the Almighty. Others suppose that these grinning creatures perched aloft on the roof and tower represent the spirits of the power of the air which endeavour to assail the faithful.

Some people imagine that these hideous figures represent evil men and women who have been ex-communicated from the Church, and others that they were carved in satire and record the disputes which arose in the Middle Ages between the monks and the parish clergy.

However, I think that our first interpretation of the meaning of gurgoyles is the best. They are intended to represent human vices, and to show how really hideous sin is.

We notice, also, how ably these quaint figures are carved. Many of them are uncouth, but they are always the best that those who carved them could do at the time, and they always contribute to the architectural effect and were of practical utility in conveying the water from the roof to the ground without injuring the walls. They are never without picturesque power, sometimes rising to grace, and sometimes sinking to ugliness, but they always add life to the whole building. Monsters gaped and grinned from waterspouts, little figures or strange animals twisted in and out of the foliage at angles and corners, but they were all intended to enforce some lesson, and to teach by the eye those spiritual truths which the men of every age so much need. The gurgoyles at Little Stukeley, in Huntingdon, are particularly horrible ; and we wonder how the fourteenth-century masons could have conceived such dreadful shapes and monsters. In the interior of this church we have the pleasing subject of a soul being devoured by the devil, who is represented as a dragon. The villagers call it Jonah swallowed by a whale.

The Norman walls were built of rubble, the smoothly chiselled ashlar work being confined to the corners, the arches of the doors, and windows and buttresses. But the masons were not satisfied with this rough building, and began to set the stones in regular order, until at length all the blocks of stone were chiselled and squared ; and though the walls were thinner, they were quite as strong as the massive rubble walls of the earlier craftsmen. It will be noticed that the mediæval builders were not content to leave the surface of the walls plain and unadorned. The Norman masons were very fond of arcading or blind arches, especially on their towers and west and east fronts, with characteristic pilasters and semicircular arches. Sometimes later in the style these arches were made to interlace, and are adorned with usual Norman mouldings, such as the zigzag, cable, indented, etc. The Early English builders also loved arcading, which was carried out in accordance with their usual style, with pointed arches and capitals, adorned with stiff-leaved foliage. In the fourteenth and fifteenth centuries the windows became so large and occupied so much space that little room was left for arcading, and this mode of decoration ceased.

Naturally, the interior surface of the walls was more highly ornamented than the exterior, which was exposed to the effects of the weather. But the men, who loved their churches, would not leave any part uncared for or destitute of that which contributed to their beauty and perfection. To break the monotony of the wall-surface they introduced a string-course, or horizontal projecting moulding, running horizontally along the wall. It has usually a rounded surface, with sometimes a fillet below, and appears on the interior walls. It generally is placed immediately below the windows, and discharges a useful function of partially protecting the lower part of the wall from the dripping rain-water running down the upper portion. It also acts as a bonding course between the part of the wall pierced by windows and that which is not pierced. The interesting church at Sompting professes to have the earliest string-course in England. Sometimes it is carried round a buttress, and completely encircles the building. Over windows and doorways there is a similar projection, called a label or hood-moulding, which has for its purpose the diverting of the streams of rain-water from the object it protects. Sometimes this label or hood-moulding is continued in a horizontal direction and forms another string-course.

Another form of decoration is the use of corbels or projecting stones, carved in the shape of heads or monsters. You see a nun with an unmistakable smile looking down upon you, or a demon grinning, or a crowned monarch, or a holy saint, carved on these stone corbels. What is their use? The old masons generally had some object for their work. We look up and see that there is a row of these corbels which support a long, flat course of stones on a parapet which slightly projects from the surface of the walls. This course of stones on the top of the corbels is called a corbel-table. Sometimes little trefoil arches spring from the corbels, and upon them the parapet rests. Occasionally we see corbels and, perhaps, a corbel-table some little distance below the top of the wall. These apparently belong to an earlier arrangement of the roof and parapet. The wall has been raised and the old corbels left in their place to tell us of this important change.

These corbels continued in fashion during the greater part of the Early English period, after which time they were abandoned in favour of a moulded projecting course of masonry that supported the parapet. Parapets do not exist in all country churches, but we find examples, richly carved and ornamented, in quite small villages, such as Ashbury, in Berkshire. In Norman times the parapet was fashioned quite plain, but later on it formed an important addition to the scheme of the decoration of the building. It was divided up into panels, and these were carved with designs, such as circles, trefoils, or quatrefoils, sometimes on the surface or in many other cases cut through in the form of pierced tracery. You see these parapets on the summit of the walls of the aisles and clerestory, projecting slightly from the surface of the walls and concealing the gutters of the roof. In Perpendicular times they were commonly battlemented, similar to those you have seen on castellated domestic buildings, whence they took their rise, and were adopted by the masons who built our churches. You will not discover such battlemented parapets in any foreign countries, as they are peculiar to our island.

Turning our eyes down to the ground, we notice

that the base of the walls projects. In some small churches, indeed, this plinth is wanting, and they look as if they were sinking into the ground, instead of springing from it. But in all dignified and well-designed edifices the plinth forms an admirable sub-structure, pleasing to the eye, and giving strength to the building. It is usually moulded, the sections showing graceful curves and corresponding with the forms peculiar to the various styles.

Occasionally we meet with a circular shallow incision in the wall, containing a cross. This is a consecration cross, of which there were originally twelve, but during the process of reconstruction, alteration, and restoration many have been lost or obliterated. When a church was consecrated twenty-four crosses were anointed with holy oil or chrism by the officiating bishop, twelve on the exterior and a like number on the interior surface of the walls of the building. The north, east, south, and west walls had each three crosses, which were carved, or otherwise prepared for the purpose, prior to the consecration ceremony. On the exterior surface of the walls these crosses were usually carved in circular incisions, and frequently a metal cross was let into the stonework. The metal has in most cases disappeared, but you can see the holes in the stonework by means of which it was attached. The interior crosses, not being exposed to the weather, were usually painted, and red was the favourite colour. During the elaborate ceremony of consecration the bishop used to anoint this cross with chrism, and was often obliged to ascend a ladder in order to reach it.

The characteristic ornament of each period proclaims the style and the age in which each particular part of the church was erected. Thus, in the Early English period the dog-tooth ornament was used profusely. This was a development of the nail-head moulding which is found in Anglo-Norman work, and which survived in the early years of the Early English period. The ball-flower is characteristic of the buildings of the Decorated period, when the masons also were very fond of carving the four-petalled flower ornaments, which also lingered on in the Perpendicular style, when the Tudor flower became the favourite form of decoration.[1]

We look up at the roof of the church. It is now low and scarcely appears above the parapet of the clerestory ; but it was not always so. You see those marks or slightly projecting triangular ridge of stonework on the eastern side of the tower. That was the height of the roof in the thirteenth century, when much of the church was built. But timbers decay, tiles fall off, and the rain gets into the beams of the roof and causes

---

[1] A fuller description of the characteristic styles, ornaments, and mouldings of each style, with illustrations, will be found in my book, *Handbook of English Gothic Architecture* (Messrs. Dent & Sons).

them to rot. Hence, in the fourteenth or fifteenth century, a new roof was required, and the builders of that period loved a flatter roof and lower elevation. So they erected the present one, covering it with lead, that was not rolled in sheets like the metal now in use, but cast in a casting-frame, and has needed little repair ever since. This lead is very valuable, and church robbers have always had a lust for lead, and at the Reformation stole much from the roofs of chantries and churches in their greedy covetousness. When this leaden roof in modern days needed repair, we have known the custodians of churches very eager to substitute slate for the ancient covering, on the same principle that a rascally blacksmith assured me that my pump was worn out, that I wanted an iron pump, which he kindly supplied, and purloined the lead of the old one, making a nice little profit. We will examine the wonderful woodwork of the roof when we enter the building.

I think we have examined all the parts of the building that are to be seen from the outside, except the porch, tower, windows, and doors, which will be described in separate chapters. All that we have seen hitherto has been mediaeval work, true Gothic, but here and there we find Renaissance details in porch or tower, if not a whole church that differs almost entirely from anything that has been described. In Italy, while Henry VIII was destroying the magnificent minsters and holy shrines of the monks, and, indeed, some years prior to that iconoclastic sacrilege, there sprang up a love for classical architecture and a revival of classicalism that laughed to scorn the so-called barbarity of Gothic art. Instead of soaring arch and lofty spire, of west-fronts gorgeous with the statues of saints, the new builders began to admire the works of the old Roman and Greek builders. They raised again great pillars of Corinthian, Doric, or Ionic character, with profusely decorated capitals surmounted by an entablature and crowned by a triangular-shaped pediment. They introduced a modification of the Corinthian order and called it the Composite, and a fifth order, which they called Tuscan, a debased form of Roman Doric. Porticoes, round-headed arches, low steeples, and fantastic spires became the fashion, and the basilica type of church found favour once more. The founders of this school in Italy called themselves Cinque-centists, and thought that they had found the ideal architecture. Some Italian masons were brought to England by Henry VIII, and the new ideas introduced by them considerably modified the native style then in vogue. This native style, the late Perpendicular or Tudor style, had developed into an extraordinary richness and superfluity of gorgeous decoration, but it remained Gothic ; and then came the foreign influence of the Renaissance, brought to the country by their Italian workmen, and contended with the native style, until in Elizabeth's time there was a combination of the two, Gothic tradition and the ideas of the Cinquecento school. Inigo Jones and Sir Christopher Wren were the apostles of this English Renaissance, whose work may be seen principally in London. In country churches, however, we find traces of their influence in porch, or doorway, or tower, or magnificent tomb, and some village churches were entirely rebuilt during the period of the highest development of Renaissance art. English people are very conservative. They cling to their accustomed traditions, and in spite of the constant importation of foreign ideas, the masons and architects of this country maintained their affection for the style handed down to them by their forefathers, and did not lightly give up their connection with a great historic past. The after-glow of Gothic is seen in many a part of England, in the beautiful Tudor houses that arose, in cottage buildings, and in Oxford, where the Somerset masons were busy building Wadham College and Lincoln College was raising its beautiful pile. Indeed, the Gothic tradition still lingers on in the Cotswold country, where the old masons build as their fathers and forefathers did before them, before Renaissance influence was felt in England, and when they were rearing the splendid fanes of Fairford and Lechlade and other triumphs of Cotswold art.

It is not to be supposed that good building

ceased with the Middle Ages, and with the last efforts of the Perpendicular builders. It is true that the masons of the latter half of the sixteenth century did not have much opportunity for exercising their skill on ecclesiastical buildings. Many of the monastic churches were saved when the monasteries disappeared, and became parochial churches. These and the older edifices sufficed for the needs of the population. The *nouveaux riches* with their coffers full of the spoils of the monasteries, and the rich merchants, instead of building churches, fashioned stupendous monuments for themselves, employing Flemish and German workmen, who added Renaissance detail to the work of the English craftsmen, and built for themselves beautiful and costly dwellings which departed little from the traditional style. However, even the best built buildings will fall into decay, and when they have been plundered and ransacked show evidences of the presence of the spoliators.

Hence, in the later years of Elizabeth's reign, and when the Stuarts came to the throne, in spite of the irreligion of the Court, efforts were made to restore churches and even to build new ones. The presence of a new style combined with the old is seen in the porch of Sunningwell Church, near Oxford, where we find rough Ionic columns and Gothic tracery. It was built in 1562. Quarrendon Church, in Buckinghamshire, was restored by Sir Henry Lee in 1600, but time has reduced it again to a few roofless arches, together with the knight's mansion and his monument. Sir Marmaduke Dayrell rebuilt Fulmer Church in the same county and added his splendid marble monument, whereon he is shown lying in gilt armour with his lady. All these show Gothic tradition with the rude attempt to copy the details of the new style which was only slowly creeping into the country districts.

These and other attempts were in progress when Laud, the future Archbishop, revived the Church's life and stimulated the desire to make the Houses of God in the land more worthy of their high spiritual uses. We can find many evidences of this new movement. As Bishop of St. David's and then of Bath and Wells, he caused much restoration in the West Country. Amongst these good works we may mention Sandbach, Astbury, Nantwich, and Barthomley, Cheshire (between the years 1620-24) ; Charing, Kent, destroyed by fire, was rebuilt about the same time, also the tower and other parts of the church of Halstead, Passenham Church, Northamptonshire, and Leighton-Bromswould, Huntingdonshire. The chapel of Groombridge, Kent, was rebuilt in 1621 ; its style is Gothic, except the porch, which bears evidences of the new style. The church at Plaxtole, Kent, is remarkable. It bears the inscription :—

THIS CHURCH WAS BYLTE FOR THE WORSHIP OF GOD,
AN. DO. 1649.

It is essentially Gothic and has not the least trace of any Renaissance work.

Although the masons in country districts were building in the old style, the carpenters had adopted the new fashions. Hence we find in many of our churches the carved woodwork in pew and pulpit which we call Jacobean, and which was mainly German in its character, having been introduced by the artisans from that country who worked here during the reign of James I. There is one church that is remarkable in that it was built during the time of the Commonwealth period, and it is believed to be the only church erected during that time of oppression. This church guards the precincts of Staunton Harold, the seat of Earl Ferrers, in Leicestershire. It stands in the beautiful park with its fine tower, and might have been built two hundred years earlier, so Gothic is its spirit and design. In the chancel there is this inscription : " Sir Robert Shirley, Baronet, founder of this church, Anno Domini MDCLIII, on whose soul God have mercy," and over the entrance appears another inscription placed there by the son of the founder, when the storm of persecution had passed away : " In the year 1653, when all things sacred throughout the nation were either demolished or profaned, Sir Robert Shirley, Baronet, founded this church, whose singular praise it is to have done the best thing in the worst times, and hoped them in the most calamitous.

The Righteous shall be had in everlasting remembrance."

Amongst the fine monuments of Renaissance art we may mention those in the churches of Ashbourne, Braybrook, Burford, Colyton, Poltimore, and Wickhampton ; and note also the font-covers of Astbury and St. Mary-the-less at Cambridge ; a fine octagonal pulpit at Netherbury, Dorset ; the rich manor pew of Holcombe, surmounted by an arcade of carved pillars and arches supporting a frieze of tablets covered with scriptural subjects. A very fine piece of Renaissance art is seen in Croscombe Church, Somerset, consisting of a screen, pulpit, and panelled pews, erected in 1616.

It is the fashion of the lovers of Gothic art to despise the achievements of the builders of this later date, and with foolish ignorance endeavour to abolish from their churches during a " restoration " the results of the labours of the Renaissance masons. They pretend that a Gothic church must be entirely Gothic, and that all subsequent work should be eliminated. There could not be a greater mistake. These classical additions form part of the history of the building. They lack not a merit of their own, and should be preserved with the same strict caution as the other parts of the church.

There is one other object to notice, and that is the masons' marks on the stonework, which have a special history, and about which much has been written. On Norman work you will often find stones marked across the surface with a delicately pointed chisel, always diagonally if the stone be flat, but following the leading lines if the work were moulded. The Early English masons made their marks with a toothed chisel, and these are upright. Usually each family of masons had its mark, the son differentiating his mark by slightly altering that of his sire. Thus a father would use a double cone for his mark, and a son would bisect it by a vertical or horizontal line. It is possible to trace the work of families of masons in different buildings by these marks, which can be found in foreign countries also. It would be a great advantage if all such marks could be carefully noted, copied, and published.

Our church is built of stone. It lies on the track of that oolite limestone which has given birth to most of the architectural triumphs of our island. In the days when transit was difficult, the builders were obliged to use the materials which Nature afforded in the particular district in which their work was situated. Where good building stone was scarce they used flints, or timber which the old forests supplied. Of the Saxon timber churches only one remains, which perhaps shows a Scandinavian element in Saxon architecture. The church at Greenstead, Essex, is not unlike the wooden churches of Norway and Sweden, and that county possesses many others in which timber is largely used. Cheshire, too, has an important group of timber-framed churches which rival in beauty the " magpies " or black and white homesteads for which that county is famous. Nether or Lower Peover, Marton, Siddington, Warburton, part of the chancel of Chadkirk, and some others constitute this group, and are described by Dr. Cox in *The Memorials of Old Cheshire*, a volume edited by Archdeacon Barber and myself. Brick, too, is used in the building of churches, especially in the seventeenth century. The roofing material also varies. Lead, tiles, slates, and even thatch cover our churches. A considerable number of East Anglian churches were formerly thatched, and Rampton, Cambridgeshire, and Thornham Parva, Suffolk, have retained this mode of roofing, which owing to the constant danger of fire and for other reasons is not the most desirable, and has often found a more excellent substitute.

Sometimes we find odd curiosities on the exterior walls of churches. As the local archers made bows of the branches of yew-trees growing in churchyards, so they sharpened their arrows on the stones of the tower, and have left the marks behind them. A coloured red line on the north wall of Llansilin Church is a relic of the time when the game of " fives " was played in the churchyard, just as the nine holes on the stone benches of the cloisters of some of our cathedrals tell of the " Nine Men's Morris " which the choirboys played when they were not busy with their studies.

Sometimes we find a canopied tomb on the exterior wall of a church, as at Aldworth, and at Bishopsteighton, and curious carving is let into the wall which is conjectured to be a Saxon representation of the Adoration of the Magi.

We have perambulated the church, but before we enter the building we must look up at the spire and learn from it its lesson of *Sursum corda* ; but that must be left to the next chapter.

The frontispiece of this book shows a view of the exterior of the beautiful and graceful church of Bottesford, near Grantham, Lincolnshire, often styled the " Lady of the Vale." It has a richly crocketed spire and an Early English chancel, transepts and porch and Perpendicular nave. It contains some remarkable monuments of the families of De Ros and Manners. On account of its singular beauty and attractiveness, I have selected it as an example of a good exterior view of a village church, though it has many rivals, and the choice for a place of honour is difficult.

CHAPTER IV

TOWERS AND SPIRES

WHEN we approach a village the first object that strikes the eye is the tower or spire of the church that rises above the trees and seems to call to us with a living voice. Ages ago, when the land was wild with woods or fenland, its tolling bell has saved some lost wanderer's life, who gratefully has left a bequest for the ringing of a bell to guide travellers lone as he to a safe anchorage. The spire points heavenwards, and yet it seems ever to keep watch and ward over the life of the village and the destiny of its people. It sympathizes with their woes, rejoices with them in their joys, and in dark days of war and rapine the tower was their place of refuge, their ark of safety. They have a wonderful individuality, these towers, and the small village church towers and spires afford quite as interesting a study as the great massive soaring structures of the great minster or cathedral.

There is a great variety of towers and spires. Sometimes there is a great square tower at the crossing of a cruciform church, which may generally be presumed to be of Norman architecture. Frequently the ambitious successors of the twelfth-century masons have superimposed an additional story, that has often tried too severely the strength of Norman masonry and foundations and caused a collapse of the whole structure. Sometimes the tower is at the west end, and there are occasional examples of detached towers, as at Berkeley ; but wherever it stands it adds dignity to the edifice and has its own striking personality.

Why did our ancestors build these towers? They served several purposes, the chief and original one being the housing of the bells. From very early times in England church bells have pealed forth their summons to the world to attend the services in the House of God, " to set their affections on things above, and not on things on the earth." They have shared, too, in national triumphs, in the loyalty to the throne, in the homage due to king or queen or bishop who visited the village, in the coming of age of the squire's son, and in degenerate days even with the winning of his racehorses. Whenever there were popular rejoicings the voice of the bells joined in the universal chorus. These bells required a suitable place for their accommodation, and one reason for the building of towers was the housing of these tuneful messengers of joy or grief.

It has been already mentioned that towers were places of refuge in unsettled times. The nobles had their castles, the villagers their church tower, whither they could retire when bands of outlaws roamed the forest lands or foes more powerful threatened their homesteads. This is specially noticeable on the borders of Wales and Scotland and in East Anglia, where there was a constant danger of incursions from sea-rovers, the descendants of the dread Vikings, who carried fire and sword into many a peaceful hamlet. In that district there are many round towers built of flint. Why they should have assumed this form has been a puzzle to architects. The mind connects them with the famous round towers of Ireland, which were certainly built as places of refuge, the entrance usually being rather high from the ground and only gained by a ladder. Hence when fightings threatened (and when did fights not threaten in Ireland?) the more peace-loving people would mount the ladder leading to their stronghold, draw it up after them, and defy the invaders. The similar structures in East Anglia do not seem to have had any connection with these Irish refuges, and were probably built of flints because no other stone was available, and round because by that arrangement the masons could dispense with the stone-built corners. We have two round towers in Berkshire, at Welford and Great Shefford, and you will find similar buildings at Little Saxham, Barsham, and Herringfleet in Suffolk, Bessingham, Haddiscoe, and Witton in

Norfolk, Snailwell and Bartlow in Cambridgeshire, and at other villages in the Eastern Counties.
There are 130 in Norfolk alone, besides 40
in Suffolk and 8 in Essex.

Sir Walter Scott's stirring line—

Half house of God—half castle 'gainst the Scot,

well describes several of these fortress towers that
exist in the Cheviot district to guard against the
coming of the northern marauding bands and
clansmen rovers. Burgh-on-Sands, where Edward I
died in 1307, near Carlisle, has an example of
these fortified churches, and Ancroft's tower, near
Berwick-on-Tweed, was prepared to resist a foe,
as was the church of Annan, on the Scottish side
of the Solway. Great Salkeld, in Cumberland,
has a church tower which was especially well
adapted for defence. The only entrance to it
is from the nave, in the interior of the building.
The door is covered with iron plates, and it is
evident that the tower was intended for a place of
refuge, as there are strong bars on the tower-side
of this door, showing that the inhabitants of the
place were in the habit of seeking shelter therein
and there defending themselves from the dreaded
Scots. In this tower was a store of armour.
Moreover, in several towers in England as far
south as Rothwell and Wakefield there are traces
of machicolations, by means of which the besieged
folk could cast down hot sand and darts and

melted lead upon the heads of the attacking force. Newton, on the Cumberland coast, is more like a fortress than a church. The doorway is only two feet seven inches wide, the windows are all high up, more than seven feet from the ground, and only a foot wide. The tower has a fireplace. Bedale Church tower is strong and massive, and had a portcullis at the foot of the staircase. The towers of the Yorkshire churches of Middleham and Melsonby are fortified structures. Bradford Church tower during the Civil War was hung with wool-packs.

At Hulne Abbey, on the Ralne, there is a detached tower, erected in 1424, which was designed as a place of refuge. Pirate raids were not infrequent on the Welsh coast. Several of the Pembrokeshire towers were built as fortresses for the purpose of resisting the foe. Such an one is to be seen at Manorbier, and on the coast of Glamorganshire there is a noble, bold, and massive tower at Newton Nottage. It is very remarkable, and is said to be unique in the British Isles. High up on its eastern face you can see jutting out from the surface of the wall certain stones which in former days supported a wooden-covered gallery. In this the defenders could find shelter and shower down their arrows and darts upon the pirates who came to attack the church. Time and weather have destroyed the woodwork, but you can still see the doorway through which the bowmen entered upon the gallery and bade defiance to their foes.

Herefordshire has several churches, the towers of which are built quite separately from the church. The Norman tower at Ledbury is separated some little distance from the church, and thus acted as a place of refuge when wild bands of Welshmen harried the border. There are bullet-holes in the church door, memorials of a skirmish fought here during the Civil War of the seventeenth century, when Rupert drove out Massey and his Roundheads. Bosbury Church, near Ledbury, has also a detached Norman tower.

Another use of the tower or spire was to act as a guide to travellers by land or sea. The church at Little Budworth, in Cheshire, has a tower, and on its summit is an iron cresset for holding 'a beacon fire. There is also one at Hadley Church, Middlesex, and some few churches have beacon turrets for the special purpose of conveying signals. In disturbed times, when an enemy threatened our coasts, before the days of electric telegraphs, it was customary to have a chain of beacon lights on the summits of high hills or church towers ; and when these were fired the people knew that danger was at hand, and they flocked to a pre-arranged rendezvous and were ready to meet the foe. This was done when the Spanish Armada threatened, as Macaulay sings in his stirring verse ; and when the Pilgrimage of Grace was formed, owing to accidental or intentional lighting of the bonfire on Pendal Hill, which caused the cressets to glow on many a tower and keep, ere yet the bands of rebels were ready, this unhappy signal was one of the causes which led to disaster.

Sailors at sea when trying to make the harbour need some prominent mark by which to steer their barks into " the haven where they would be."　Hence a fine tall spire is very useful to them, and the high-soaring Boston " stump " was reared to guide them to a safe anchorage. On its summit is an octagonal open lantern, supported by four flying buttresses, springing from lofty pinnacles at the angles of the tower. In this a beacon light used to guide mariners entering the River Witham from the Wash. Boston is not a village, and therefore its church does not come within the scope of this book ; but many a Lincolnshire village can boast of a high-towering spire, which served as a guide to seamen or to the travellers who had to find their way through the dismal fen country.

The construction of towers varies with the material produced by Nature in the neighbourhood wherein the church is situate. In our own district of Windsor Forest timber often forms the main material of which the towers are constructed. The king used to grant to the inhabitants gifts of a hundred oaks for building or repairing a church or a tower, and massive great beams form the construction of the place for the bells. An example of this may be seen in the church of Swallowfield, which was built by Sir John Le Despencer in 1256 by the special authority of Pope Alexander IV, conveyed by two Bulls in response to a petition of the knight, who pleaded the danger which he and his family had to encounter, in going through the forest to Mass at the church of Sonning, from robbers in summer and floods in winter. This timber belfry is a very fine specimen of its kind, and there was another at my own church at Barkham until the " Goths and Vandals " of the nineteenth century pulled it down and erected another in the Victorian Gothic style.

Towers of stone existed in Saxon times, and many examples are left to us which have survived the rest of the buildings erected in that period. They are usually lofty and slender in proportion, very different from the low, massive towers of the Norman period. They usually stand at the west end, and may be recognized by several important characteristics. The " long and short work " at the corners—that is to say, the alternate use of stones set vertically and horizontally—is usually deemed to be a hall-mark of Saxon work, and was certainly extensively used by them, though in districts where stone was scarce this method of laying stone was adopted in later times. You can see this very clearly in the tower of Earl's

Barton Church, in Northamptonshire, and in many other Saxon towers. Another characteristic is the peculiar shape of the sound-openings, through which the sweet music of the bells sent forth their tender message to the world. These consist of round-headed openings, divided by baluster shafts—*i.e.* a stone shaft resembling a wooden one that had been turned in a lathe. Usually this opening consists of two lights divided by the shaft, the arches being flush with the surface of the wall. Examples of these openings may be seen at Wickham (Berkshire), Northleigh (Oxon), Bolam and Billingham (Durham), Hornby (Yorks), and there are several others.

Another characteristic of Saxon towers is the ornamentation on the surface of the walls by the use of pilaster strips, consisting of slightly projecting vertical strips of stone, such as we see in the highly decorated tower at Earl's Barton. It is possible that in this, as in the case of the baluster shaft, the builders preserved some memory of early timber belfries, and imitated in stone the structures fashioned of wood. In some instances the masons seem to have cut out these pilasters after the tower was built, as they did at Bradford-on-Avon. Some authorities attribute this form of decoration to an imitation of later Roman models.

These Saxon masons were no mean craftsmen. They built surely and well. They had confidence in the stability of these towers, a confidence which their endurance through many centuries proves was not misplaced ; and therefore they did not deem it necessary to support them with strong buttresses. We know not how their towers were crowned. Many of them have embattled parapets and pinnacles ; but these are all of later design and are additions. But one church in England reveals what may have been a common practice. I refer to the little church at Sompting, in Sussex, which has a Saxon tower, each face of which terminates in a gable, and the whole is crowned by a short four-sided spire made of timber and covered with tiles. Such may have been the usual type of tower roofing in Saxon days. At any rate, it exists in this Sussex church, which has many attractions.

Such are some of the principal features of a Saxon tower. But soon the Norman conquerors came, and with their advent a new era of church building dawned. Norman towers differ greatly from their Saxon predecessors. As we have seen, they usually occupy a central position, and were low and squat. The splendid Norman churches at Iffley and Stewkley furnish examples of central towers, even when the church is not cruciform and has no transepts. An external turret with a circular stair provides access to the ringing chamber, and there is often an arcade composed of round-headed arches breaking the surface of the walls, and some of these are pierced with windows to give light to the belfry or as sound holes. These arches partake of the nature of the usual Norman type, and are recessed and adorned with mouldings and are supported by pilaster shafts. Few of these towers have escaped the attention of subsequent builders, who have often capped them with another story, and thereby tried the strength of the foundations, which, in spite of the appearance of Norman massiveness, were not very secure. Hence many have fallen and brought destruction upon the neighbouring parts of the nave and choir and transept, necessitating a rebuilding. Hence we find, as at Waltham St. Lawrence, the western arches of the nave arcade pure Norman, whereas the eastern were rebuilt in the fourteenth century, indicating doubtless the collapse of a central tower. Where the later builders did not impose a heavy superstructure they added pinnacles at the four corners or an embattled parapet, or filled the windows with tracery, every attempt being made to improve and beautify the House of God, but often disguising the original work of their predecessors. In these days we are often accused of not reverencing the work of our ancestors and of trying to improve upon it. Such is the conceit of men in all ages, and the attempt is worthy, if the results are not always satisfactory. The twelfth-century tower, when it has not been altered, was probably capped by a cone-shaped squat spire or simply roofed over, showing two gable-ends, as at Castle Rising, in Norfolk.

When soaring Gothic supplanted massive Romanesque and Early English masons were constructing their beautiful buildings, realizing half-unconsciously the aspirations and longings of ages, the tower and spire soared higher and assumed more graceful proportions. They became the expression of the Gothic spirit when wearied with the uncouth Romanesque details of Norman art ; the masons of England and France were feeling after and finding a more excellent way and devising lighter and more elegant forms of construction and decoration. The tower windows accorded with the fashion of the style, which has been described already, and the spire began to rear its lofty head and disclose its gracefulness and beauty. It owed its origin and inspiration to the square pyramid that capped many a Norman tower. It was fashioned sometimes of timber and sometimes of stone, and was usually of the type we call a broach spire—that is to say, it capped the tower and did not spring from within a parapet. The broach spire was like an elongated roof ; usually in its upper portion it was octagonal, and was connected with the square summit of the tower at the four corners by half pyramids. Thus ingeniously did the masons fit an eight-sided sloping structure on a square base. These spires often had windows jutting out on the north, south, east, and west faces in the form of dormers, and occasionally pinnacles stand at the four corners of the tower ; but these are more usual in those built in a later period. Examples of these beautiful Early English towers may be seen at Sleaford, Lincolnshire ; Horsham, Sussex ; Warmington, Northants ; and many other villages throughout the country.

In the next century, when Decorated architecture prevailed, and the era of the greatest beauty of English art set in, the tower and spire partook of the greater elaborations of detail and ornament which characterized that style. This is especially evident in the windows and belfry openings, and in the adornment of the angular buttresses which now became a feature of the structure and projected farther from the wall than in the preceding ages. The spire now springs from within the parapet, and pinnacles arise, not only at the four corners of the tower, but at the base of the spire, forming a graceful cluster. Bands of ornament adorn its surface, and crocketed ribs, often adorned with the ball-flower, run up the ridges of the spire. The parapet is often adorned with open-worked tracery, and is frequently embattled. The triumphs of these Decorated spires and towers are usually found in towns and cities, such as Oxford, where that of St. Mary's is a glorious example of rich and beautiful design ; but many a fair and graceful spire of this period rises in quite small

E

villages, and, set in its framework of trees, gives a charm to the hamlet and is a continual sign and token of religious aspiration and endeavour.

Towers raised in the Perpendicular style of architecture during the fifteenth and early sixteenth centuries are very numerous, and the builders were usually content to raise a tower elaborately ornamented and adorned with crocketed pinnacles and parapets without adding a soaring spire. These pinnacles were multiplied, and appear not only at the corners, but at the centre of each face, and sometimes are more numerous still, forming a fine group. The masons of the period were very proud of their panelling design, which is the hall-mark of the Perpendicular style. They covered the surface of the walls of their towers with these panels. The Norfolk builders sometimes placed statues of saints in place of the pinnacles at the top of the tower, and were very fond of the four Latin doctors of the Church, SS. Jerome, Ambrose, Gregory, and Augustine, who appear in this position. Sometimes the four evangelists are represented. The symbol of the saint to whom the church is dedicated sometimes appears in Norfolk churches in the ornamental work of the base or battlements of the tower.[1]

Buttresses are adorned with niches for statues. Great windows with their panelled tracery look out from the western front and from the belfry

[1] *Norfolk Churches*, by Dr. Cox.

stage, and central towers have large windows on each face. Though spires are less common than in the preceding style there are some of the finest in England which belong to this period, and some of them are in small villages. Owing to the dislocation of trade caused by the introduction of steam-driven machinery, villages that are now quite small were in olden days large and important centres of industry, when the making of cloth was carried on in them, and there were guilds and woolmen and fairs and markets, and all the bustle and prosperity of a flourishing manufacturing centre. Hence the inhabitants devoted their wealth and their interest to their church and made it a large and beautiful building, which still stands, though the looms are all gone and a few rustics are only left to worship there. Such a church is Thaxted in Essex, and there are many other villages which have noble churches but very small communities.

These Perpendicular spires are graceful, slender, crocketed structures with pinnacles richly adorned with panels and crockets, and flying buttresses connect them with the spire, the ribs of which are adorned with crockets, and a fine vane crowns the summit. In some of the bigger churches an octagonal lantern takes the place of the spire. Sometimes towers are endowed with a personality, similar to that bestowed on bells. At Colbourne in the Isle of Wight a tablet states " I am risen from ye Ruins of near 70 years."

Some localities developed special styles of tower building. A very distinctive and remarkable one is observed in Somerset, which owes partially its superiority to the abundance and variety of local building materials. The late Mr. B. E. Ferrey, F.S.A., wrote thus in the *Proceedings of the Somerset Archæological Society:*—

Though some of the quarries of the " Bath " stone are not actually in Somerset, they are so near the border that, with the others, they take their name from it. In the county is Doulting stone, used at Wells Cathedral and Glastonbury Abbey, a wonderfully durable material ; Ham Hill stone, ruddy looking in its youth, calm-looking and grey, covered with lovely-tinted lichens, in its old age ; the red sandstone of Bishop's Lydeard and the neighbourhood ; the sober-coloured blue lias, too often, alas ! treacherous and undurable, but forming the excellent paving-stones and steps of Keinton and Street ; and the Pennant, quarried near Bristol. The blue lias also produces that splendid material, the lime of Watchet, almost equal in strength to Portland cement. Then there is the white lias, such as is found in the neighbourhood of Wells and Shepton Mallet, resembling Caen stone in its white colour and texture. This is the same employed in the sculpture of the arch mouldings to the west front of Wells Cathedral. Then last, though not least, there is that rich purplish-red conglomerate, or pudding-stone, called Draycott, which will take a half-polish like marble ; and the semi-freestone of Wedmore may be added.

With such a variety of material wonderful results have been obtained, especially when the buildings are set in such wonderful scenes of rural beauty, some having for their background the dark ranges of the Mendips, and others the rounded hills of Quantock and Brendon, or the wooded spurs of Exmoor, or the green pastures between Glastonbury and Langport. These Somerset towers usually stand at the west end, are square in plan and unadorned by spires. They are nearly all of fifteenth or sixteenth century construction, and show an astonishing variety, which is due, not to any difference of style, but solely to individuality of treatment. As a recent writer has said : " Abundant evidence is shown of the versatility and resource of the builders, all the more striking as being displayed at a time when Gothic architecture was already on the wane, and when its decline had actually begun elsewhere."

These Somerset builders paid great attention to their towers and glorified them exceedingly. This was not due only to the good building material, nor to the fact that they were wanted for the accommodation of good peals of bells, which rang merrily at that time in the West Country ; but rather to the influence of the grand architectural beauties of Wells and Glastonbury, and to the friendly rivalry of neighbouring parishes, which strove to make their towers as fair and strong and beautiful as the art and skill of men could accomplish. Such are the towers of Staple Fitzpaine, Shepton Mallet, Evercreech, Cheddar, Huish Episcopi, and Ilminster. Parapets are pierced with geometrical patterns, and open tracery work is commonly used in the battlements and pinnacles. Slender pinnacles based on corbels are attached by little flying buttresses to the corner pinnacles. The walls are decorated with blind tracery, and canopied niches with statues and horizontal bands of ornament unite to give distinction to these Somerset towers.

In the neighbouring county of Devon the stone used is the hard red sandstone, which is so difficult to carve that the masons were obliged to leave them plain and unadorned. They did not try to fashion elaborate pinnacles, and sometimes left them out altogether. They were merciful to elderly ringers, and made the turret-stairs leading to the belfry a large and important feature of the tower. They built their towers firm and strong, and had no need to give support to them by projecting buttresses, and were quite content to leave them without adding these supports merely as ornaments. Nor did they insert many lights and windows. These Devonshire towers look stern and fortress-like, and might be descendants of those towers of refuge which bade defiance to piratical hordes in earlier days.

East Anglian churches have some peculiar towers. We have already alluded to the absence of good building stone in Eastern England and the plentifulness of flints. Hence most of these church towers are built of flint with stone dressings. They might have been framed on the model of timber houses, the dressed stone supplying the place of the timber, and the dressed flints the panels. Sometimes the alternate stone and flint form a chess - board pattern. Like the Devonshire churches, these churches usually lack pinnacles, and the buttresses are short and extend not above the belfry stage. Spires are few—at least, those built of stone ; but small, lead-covered wooden spirelets are not uncommon.

One of the objects of tower-buildings was to provide accommodation for the bells, and our forefathers, like ourselves, were keen bellringers. As we shall see presently, they rang peals on all sorts of occasions, though not, as some modern folk did, when the racehorse of a popular squire won the Derby. But they rang to celebrate all national victories and local rejoicings, the visit of a bishop or a great man. Queen Elizabeth travelled so much that the church bells would often be ringing, and then, of course, there were the ordinary services, which required a good peal. Hence our towers began to feel the effect of so much ringing, and not a few became insecure, and had to be taken down. It is not, therefore, unusual to see a good brick seventeenth-century tower built at the west end of a church. Some of these late towers are admirably constructed. There is a very fine one at Plumstead, built at the end of the reign of James I ; it is one of the most satisfactory architectural efforts of the period. Its walls are of mellowed red brick, and it is essentially Gothic. The stages rise in a graceful manner, one out of the other ; the moulded brick-work of the cornices and the window dressings show Renaissance detail, and have been skilfully designed, and the whole is comparable to work of the best period.[1] Here, in Berkshire, in the neighbourhood in which I am writing, we have examples of these late towers—at Finchampstead, where most of the church is Norman, at Ruscombe and Hurst, towers that bear witness to the capabilities of their builders, and also to the strenuousness of our ringers, whose achievements and implements we will consider in the next chapter.

[1] A drawing and description of this church are given in *Memorials of Old Kent*, by J. Tavener-Perry.

CHAPTER V

CHURCH BELLS

HIGH up in the dusty belfry the bells swing to and fro with unwearying zeal, sending forth their sweet music to the world and calling the villagers to their House of God, or proclaiming some great cause of national rejoicing, or, with muffled voice, the departure of some loved soul from earth, echoing the lamentations of his dear ones. Few ascend the well-worn belfry stairs to visit the bells, which have a long story to tell of the past life of the village and of the art of making and ringing them. English folk have always been fond of ringing their bells, and in the Middle Ages won for their country the title of the " ringing island." Other countries can boast of larger bells, but peal-ringing is peculiar to England. It was not, however, until the seventeenth century that change-ringing came into fashion, and our old bells suffered much at the hands of the enthusiastic followers of the new art. Moreover, as we have seen, it often nearly brought down the tower about their ears and necessitated the rebuilding of the belfry.

Bell-lore has many interesting branches. Ringing customs throw light upon the manners and habits of our forefathers. As the bell " Roland " at Ghent seemed endowed with a human voice, and was silenced by the Emperor Charles V lest it should again rouse the citizens to arms, so these bells in our village steeples seem to speak with living tongues and tell the story of our village life.

We need not concern ourselves about the antiquity of bells. Specimens of little bells have been found in ancient barrows of British times, and are of a globular or spheroidal form. Larger bells were made by riveting together two bent sheets of iron or bronze, like a Swiss cattle-bell, and then dipping them into molten copper or bronze. A musical note of no very great excellence can be produced from this primitive bell. One of them was found at Marden in Herefordshire, and another, called " Clog-na-fulla," or " Bell of Blood," was seen by Canon Raven in Ireland. Odoceus, Bishop of Llandaff in 550 A.D., is said to have taken the bells away from his cathedral during the time of an excommunication, and a successor of his had a bell that " exceeded every organ in sweetness of sound ; it condemned the perjured, it healed the sick, it sounded every hour without any one moving it." Unfortunately, it was touched by the polluted hands of a sinner, and henceforth ceased to sound forth its sweet message.   Indeed, it must have been a wondrous bell.

In Saxon times the architectural evidence of the existence of towers proclaims the use of bells, and the Venerable Bede tells a charming story of the sounding of a bell announcing the passing away of the holy Abbess Hilda of Whitby, that was heard thirteen miles away by Saint Begu, of the nunnery of Hackness.   In 680 St. Benedict, Abbot of Wearmouth, imported some bells from Italy.   At Crowland Abbey the bells pealed forth ; a great one called " Guthlac " after the hermit who first established his cell there, was fashioned by Abbot Turketyl, and six more by his nephew, Abbot Egelric.   Of this peal Ingulphus tells us that there was not so great a concourse of bells in the whole of England, showing that peals of bells were not unknown elsewhere.   Thomas Fuller says that the sound of this bell " Guthlac " was a sure cure for the headache ; alas ! we degenerate moderns complain that bell-ringing produces it.

Of Norman bells we know little, but as the thirteenth century dawns we get a glimpse of the progress of the art of bell-founding, in which the monks led the way.   Canon Raven tells us of one Walter de Odyngton, a monk of Evesham, who wrote a treatise on the subject of making bells in the reign of Henry III.   There is in existence at Caversfield a very early bell that was originally fashioned—it has been recast—about 1210.   This is a sanctus bell and was given, according to an inscription deciphered by Mr. Cocks, the author of the *Church Bells of Buckinghamshire*, by Hugh Gargate and Sibilla his wife. Bell-foundries were established in the same century at Lichfield, Cambridge, Paignton in Tor Bay, King's Lynn, and Bridgewater. In quite small places foundries were in existence. Close to where I am writing at Wokingham there was a noted foundry, all traces of which have disappeared, save that one road is called in the vernacular Bell Lane, and this tradition has doubtless preserved the site of the works. This foundry was busy making bells about 1360, and there are at least nine in existence at the present day which owe their origin to it. One of them hangs in the neighbouring tower of Arborfield, and I hear its sweet note every Sunday morning as in conjunction with its fellows it sends forth its melodious voice. One of the other bells in the same ring was made when the Armada was threatening our shores in the days of Queen Bess.

Bell-makers were very proud of their work, and loved to adorn their bells with decorative designs and marks by which the founders could be known. Artistic feeling pervaded the workshop and showed itself in the initial crosses, word stops, lettering, and foundry marks. The Wokingham foundry used the mark of a lion's head, an initial cross of fleurs-de-lis, and the figure of a dragon, which appears on a bell at Dorchester. This bears the inscription :—

✠ *PROTEGE* : *BIRINE* : QUOS : *CONVOCO* : TU : SINE : FINE : RAF : RASTWOLD [1]

It was a common custom to dedicate bells to saints, and the bell was supposed to be personified and to call people to church with a living voice.

A very favourite dedication was to the Blessed Virgin Mary. There was one bell called after her in the peal at Ely, the others being named Peter, John, Jesu, Walsyngham, and Bounce ; and another at Ewelme, and one at Carlisle Cathedral, which bears the inscription :—

+ 𝔍𝔥𝔠. + in : voce : sum munda : maria : sonando : secunda

which has been translated :—

> I, Mary, with pure accent sing
> Second in the chiming ring.

The Virgin is sometimes called " Star of the Sea," *Stella Maria Maris*. There is a St. Anthony at Garboldisham ; St. Margaret and St. Andrew at Lynn ; St. Paul at Warblington ; St. Catherine at Clapham, Sussex ; Chickney, Essex ; and Warfield, Berkshire ; St. George at Radclive in Bucking-

---

[1] *Victoria History of Berkshire :* chapter on the Bell Founders of the County, by J. H. Cocks, author of the *Church Bells of Bucks.*

hamshire. According to an old chartulary the bells of the priory of Little Dunmow, in Essex, were new cast and baptized in 1501, and were as follows :—

> Prima in honore Sancti Michaelis Archangeli.
> Secunda in honore Sancti Johannis Evangelisti.
> Tertia in honore S. Johannis Baptisti.
> Quarta in honore Assumptionis beatæ Mariæ.
> Quinta in honore Sanctæ Trinitatis et omnium sanctorum.

The tenor bell at Welford, Berkshire, has the inscription :—

> Missi de celis habeo nomen Gabrielis 1596.

The Angel Gabriel's name appears on many bells, and very occasionally that of Raphael. Sometimes the names of the Early Fathers appear, St. Clement, St. Ambrose, St. Augustine. After the name of a saint often appear the words, " Ora Pro Nobis," or, as it occurs on one bell, inscribed by a poor Latinist, " Horapronobis." Then we have recorded St. Lucy, St. Etheldreda, St. Edmund, St. Vincent, St. Giles, St. Martin, St. Lawrence, and almost every saint in the calendar is duly honoured in some bell inscription and dedication.

The learned in bell-lore can trace the founders' names from the marks, inscriptions, and ornaments that the bells bear. It would be vain to attempt in this chapter to enumerate all these makers and their marks, but some examples of the stamps of

LONDON FOUNDERS' MARKS, AND SHIELD OF THOMAS BALLISDON

founders may be useful in order that when you ascend the dusty belfry of your village church you may know for what to look ; and then, comparing the marks, of which you have taken rubbings, with those shown in bell-books of your county, you will be able to discover where the bells were fashioned. It is true that the bells of every shire have not yet found their chronicler, but much good work has been done in this department of antiquarian research, and ere long every county will have its campanologist.

We give an illustration of the stamp of Thomas Ballisdon, of London, who supplied many bells in the early days of the sixteenth century. He appropriately shows for his mark a hanging bell and the initials T. and B. on each side. The other figures also show the stamps of some London founders. Canon Raven in his book on *The Bells of England* describes some of the excellent work of the Norwich founders, and reproduces numerous examples of their marks, the initial letter, the rhyme stop, and the foundry shields. The " ring and cross " stamp shows the work of Richard Hille, who died in 1440, after a successful career at Faversham, and his daughter married one Henry Jordan, whose shield shows a variety of objects—cross-keys, a dolphin, a laver, a wheatsheaf, and a bell. One John Kebyll, a London founder at the end of the fifteenth century, used as his stamp the Evangelistic emblems ; and

William Culverden had an elaborate mark, a bell surmounted by a cross with the motto *In Domino fido*, and his initial W. with a rebus for his name, a dove with the letters *de* over it.

In addition to stamps and inscriptions the old founders often imprinted some quaint Latin hexameter verses on their bells, and others indulge in leonine verses, in which the first and second half rhyme. They are so called from one Leoninus, a monk of Marseilles, who lived in the early part of the twelfth century.[1] Some of them are very poor specimens of Latinity and often refuse to scan. A few examples of them will suffice :—

> Est michi collatum ihc illud nomen amætum.
> Protege Virgo pia quos convoco Sancta Maria.
> Voce mea viva depello cuncta nocina.

This last line refers to the belief that the ringing of bells drives away all demons and tempests, storms and thunder, and all other hurtful things. One bell proudly asserts :—

> Me melior vere non est campana sub ære.
> O cidus celi Barbara crimina deli.
> Martiris Eadmundi jussum decus hic ita fundi.
> Anselmi donis donum manus aptat Hugonis.

The following lines have been often quoted, and

[1] Others attribute the invention to Leonius, a canon of St. Benedict in Paris, and some to Pope Leo II in the seventh century.

tell of the many uses of the bell, including that of driving away evil :—

Laudo Deum verum, plebem voco, congrego clerum,
Funera plango, fulgura frango, Sabbata pango,
Defunctos ploro, pestem fugo, festa decoro.

A Rutland bell has the following beautiful inscription :—

Non clamor sed amor cantat in aure Dei.

Sometimes the makers liked to puzzle posterity. The fifth bell in Balsham Church has an interesting inscription, viz. :—

Non sono *subamina* mortuorum sed *subirua* viventium.

This makes nonsense, but if you read the two words italicized backwards, the translation then runs :—

I sound not forth to the souls of the dead, but to the ears of the living.

The Reformation sealed the fate of many bells, which were taken down, broken, and sold, with other Church goods in sacrilegious times, when nothing, however holy, was safe from Henry's hungry courtiers, and when churchwardens often sold their treasures lest these should fall into the hands of the King's Commissioners. The art also for a time fell into abeyance ; but soon the bell-founders were busy again, and many new names appear on bells. English, too, was used in the

F

inscriptions, and the makers frequently showed a certain ponderous humour in devising them.

They liked, also, to immortalize their names upon the work of their hands, and we constantly find such inscriptions as :—

William Knight made me,

or—

Hew Watts made me 1563,

wherein the bell is supposed to speak and bear witness to its maker's fame. Other bells keep in grateful remembrance the names of their donors.

They have a habit of boasting on their bells. One in Somerset complacently records :—

My treble voice
Makes hearts rejoice.

A bell at Combe in the same county says :—

My sound is good, my shape is neat,
'Twas Bayley made me so compleat,

and thereby sings not only its own praise, but that of its founder. Another complacent bell asserts :—

If you have a judicious ear,
You'll own my voice is sweet and clear.

Yet another joins in the chorus :—

I am the first, although but small,
I will be heard above you all.

A curious specimen of poor verse appears on the tenor of St. Benedict's, Cambridge, and runs as follows :—

> John Draper made me in 1618
> This bell was broake and cast againe
> As plainly doth appeare.
> Wich time churchwardens were
> Edwarde Dixson for the one whoe stode close to his tacklin,
> And he that was his partner then was Alexander Jacklin.

A bell that has been recast sometimes praises the merits of its new founder at the expense of its first maker. There was a celebrated foundry at Stamford, Lincolnshire, which was carried on by the Norris family, and then by Alexander Rigby. One of his bells went so far as Badgeworth in Gloucestershire, where it seems not to have given universal satisfaction. At any rate, Abel Rudhall, who recast it, inscribed on it the lines :—

> Badgworth ringers they are mad,
> Because Rigbe made me bad ;
> But Abel Rudhall you may see
> Hath made me better than Rigbe.

This Abel Rudhall was a Gloucester founder, who flourished at the beginning of the eighteenth century, and made excellent bells, which still send forth sweet sounds in places so far afield as London (St. Martin's-in-the-Fields), Manchester, Macclesfield, Bristol, Shrewsbury, and elsewhere.

These humorous rhymes are a poor substitute

for the deeply religious inscriptions which adorn the " ancients," or mediaeval bells, and one wonders how the custodians of our churches permitted such uncouth pleasantries to be perpetrated upon the musical messengers that summoned people to the sanctuary.   It is at least more appropriate to let the bells say *Sancti Paule ora pro nobis*, than to proclaim the generosity of gentlemen who contributed to their re-casting, as at Binstead, where the bell says :—

> Dr. Nicholas gave five pounds
> To help cast this peal tuneable and sound.

The bell at Alderton sounds the same tribute to its maker :—

> I'm given here to make a peal,
> And sound the praise of Mary Neale.

To such self-laudation we prefer such inscriptions as, " Laus et Gloria Deo," " Sit nomen IHC benedictum," " Laus Deo Gratia Benefactoribus," and similar expressions of praise and thanksgiving. Contrast these with sundry West Country inscriptions recorded in Canon Raven's book, such as—

> Bilbie the Founder. Bush the Hanger.
> Heathfield's the man that rings the tenor ;

or—

> Billy and Boosh may come and see
> What Evans and Nott have done for me, 1758 ;

or—

> Before I was broke I was as good as aney,
> But when that Cokey casted I near was worth a penny.

If you would like to learn all about these Bilbies and Evans and Cockeys, famous founders in their day, you must read *The Bells of England*, by the author just named, who seems to have known intimately every artist who fashioned a bell, and almost every product from their foundries.

The bells often sound forth from the village steeple, and no music delights one more in the sweet air of the country than their mellowed peal. Most sweetly do they sound on a Christmas morning when the ground is hard with frost and the rime is on the trees, and the village assumes its most picturesque garb, fairer even than in its wealth of summer glory. We ring our bells, of course, to call our people to God's House, or to give a cheerful greeting to the rustic bride and her man ere they start together on life's journey ; and when death knocks at the door of farm or cot the passing bell sounds forth and bids the neighbours pray for the soul of him who is going on a longer journey than the bridal pair. Sometimes we ring (or used to ring) the harvest bell at break of day, and the gleaners' bell to tell them when they may start gleaning after the reapers. To usher in the New Year a midnight peal is rung in many places, and the curfew is not yet silenced by the so-called march of progress. There are many other bell-ringing customs, which I have already recorded in my book on *Old English Customs,* and need not repeat here.

Not long ago we showed our loyalty by ringing peals on " Oak-Apple Day " to thank the Almighty for the deliverance of a king, and on Guy Fawkes' Day for the rescue of another king and his Parliament, though some of us in the country forget which king it was and why we ring bells and let off fireworks, while the blacksmith with a little gunpowder fires off his anvil as though it were a miniature cannon. We ring our bells, too, on wild winter evenings, sometimes because some good charitable person, like Richard Palmer, of Wokingham, left a bequest to pay the sexton for his trouble, when lands were unenclosed and forests and wild moors abounded, to guide belated travellers to their homes or to the comforts of a good inn.

Outside the church at the apex of the chancel arch or on the tower is a little bell-cot, wherein the sanctus or saunce bell once hung. This was rung during the service of the Mass when the *Ter Sanctus* was sung, in order that those who were engaged at their work might know when the canon of the Mass was about to begin, and kneel and pray to God. I have seen the arrangement for pulling this bell at Bosham Church, which used to invite the fishermen to unite in spirit with those within the church in their devotions. It is said that when George Herbert's sanctus bell sounded for prayers, the ploughmen stopped from their work for a few moments and prayed. The sanctus bell is not the same as the sacring bell, which was a hand-bell rung inside the church at the elevation of the Host.

The belfry has its laws and rules for the governance of the ringers, and these are often set forth in quaint rhyme, inscribed on a board and hung in the ringing chamber.

The following lines appear at Hastings :—

> This is a belfry that is free
> For all those that civil be;
> And if you please to chime or ring
> It is a very pleasant thing.
>
> There is no music play'd or sung
> Like unto bells when they're well rung;
> Then ring your bells well, if you can,
> Silence is best for every man.
>
> But if you ring in spur or hat,
> Sixpence you pay, be sure of that;
> And if a bell you overthrow,
> Pray pay a groat before you go.—1756.

According to most of these rules, very amusingly recorded in doggerel verse, fines were strictly levied for swearing, wearing a hat or spurs, throwing a bell, for non-attendance at practice nights, making a noise, marring a peal, sixpence being the usual amount :—

'Twill make him cautious 'gainst another time.

A ringer at Hathersage, Yorkshire, suffered hard usage if he refused to pay his fine, according to some rules that date back to 1660 :—

But whoso doth these orders disobey,
Unto the stocks we will take him straightway,
There to remain until he be willing
To pay his forfeit and the clerk a shilling.

The fines so levied were often spent in ale for the refreshment of the ringers, who thought nothing of making the belfry a tippling place. Special jugs were used to fetch the ale from the inn, and are called " ringers' jugs." Some of these remain. There is one at Hadleigh which holds sixteen quarts, and is inscribed with certain names of the ringers and the lines :—

If you love me doe not lend me,
Euse me often, and keep me clenly,
Fill me up or not at all,
If it be strong, and not with small.

Similar vessels exist at Clare, Hinderclay, and a few other places.

It is time to leave the belfry and to find our way carefully down the winding stone staircase, where the steps are worn by the feet of many ringers of former days and weary sextons, who delighted to ring the merry peal and hear the music of the bells. Their modern successors are no less skilful, keep better order in the belfry, and, instructed by the teaching of the various Guilds of Ringers, strive to make the ringing of the bells a real religious work, to carefully study the mysteries of Grandsire Tripples, Bob Major, and Treble Bobs, and—

Ring out their merry ding-dong bell.

CHAPTER VI

THE PORCH

THE entrance to the church was always regarded by our forefathers as very sacred,
and it was protected and guarded by a
building, which was called a *porticus*, or porch.
This was not merely an outside vestibule, a place
wherein to leave wet umbrellas on a rainy day,
but a distinct part of the sacred building, which
had its liturgical uses. Quite as much care was
therefore bestowed upon it as upon the rest of the
edifice. This was so even in very early times.
The remains of the little church of the basilican
type at Silchester show that in front of the church
farthest removed from the altar (that is to say, the
west end, but at Silchester the altar was at the
west end, the priest standing on the west side of
the altar and looking towards the east when he
officiated) there was an open space called the
atrium, wherein there was a well or fountain,
signifying the need of purification for all who
would enter the sanctuary ; and then there was
a *narthex*, or covered porch, open to the atrium,
and usually communicating with it by three arches.

This traditional arrangement is seen at Peterborough Cathedral and at Lincoln, forming a triple porch, and also in the little church at Snettisham.

However, most of our porches protect the south or north entrance to the nave, and, as I have said, had their liturgical uses. In very early times it is probable that the font was placed in the porch, and when later on it was removed into the church, though still placed near the door, in mediæval times the priest received the sponsors with the infant in the porch, breathed upon it and administered salt, and then led the way into the church for the performance of the full rite of baptism.

Penitents, too, assembled in the porch and there received the benefit of absolution before they were allowed to enter the church to receive the sacred mysteries. There women knelt to be churched after the birth of a child, and weddings took place, the happy pair on the conclusion of the ceremony proceeding to the altar to partake together in Holy Communion. In Myrc's *Instructions to Parish Priests* there is the following evidence of this custom :—

> Then let them come and witness bring
> To stand by at their wedding ;
> So openly at the church door
> Let them either wed the other.

Nor did the custom of weddings at the church door cease when the Reformation wrought changes in ritual and practice. As late as 1648 Robert Herrick wrote the following lines :—

The Entertainment ; or Porch Verse at the marriage of Mr. Henry Northley and the most witty Mrs. Lettice Yard.

Welcome ! but yet no entrance till we blesse
First you, then you, and both for white successe :
Profane no Porch, young Man and Maid, for fear
Ye wrong the Threshold-God that keeps peace here :
Please Him and then all good Luck will betide
You the brisk Bridegroom, you the dainty Bride.

As with baptisms and marriages, so was the porch connected with the last rite of all, and burials often took place within it. There are many other uses and ceremonies connected with the porch. It was one of the stations of the processions on Palm Sunday. Criminals sought sanctuary therein, and on fair-days stalls were set up in the porch until stringent regulations forbad the unseemly practice.

The actual building declares its age. Norman porches are usually shallow, and the masons of the twelfth century often contented themselves with their fine recessed doorways. There are some notable exceptions, such as Southwell and Malmesbury, but these are large and important churches, with which we need not concern ourselves. In ordinary village churches, if there be a Norman porch it is shallow ; nor in the Early English period do they assume large proportions ; at least in the earlier years of the thirteenth century.

Later in that period they began to increase in size and to afford protection from the weather for the carvings and mouldings of the doorways. They were built of stone, and sometimes have a groined roof and an outer doorway embellished with mouldings springing from Early English shafts.

There is an interesting porch of this date at Great Tew, in Oxfordshire. On the gable there is a short, plain-chamfered Latin cross. The outer arch has two orders, the inner rests on a bracket ; the abacus has a half roll and fillet, throating, and bead, and the vertical line a hollow chamfer and fillet-roll, throating, a small semicircular fillet, then chamfered off to the jamb. The abacus is continued to the label, which is square and chamfered. The jamb is chamfered outside to within a foot and a half from the ground. In the west wall of the porch is a double Early English window, now blocked up, with plain chamfer on the jamb and arches, which latter rest on a central rude octagonal cap, chamfered above, flat on the face, slightly undercut. The shape is circular, with a double-chamfered band at the base, and this is square, chamfered and set as a flat sill. The stone seats are of two tiers ; the inner and upper seat has a nosing and hollow chamfer with a plain-chamfered plinth, and is two feet high and one foot above the lower, which was doubtless intended for the use of children.

Uffington Church, Berkshire, has a porch of this period on the south. It has stone groining ribs springing from shafts with rounded capitals in the four corners. The outer arch is very fine, with central and side orders on each face, divided into several small roll and filleted mouldings with deep hollows between. These rest on shafts with rich conventional foliage on the capitals. There is a small shaft between the two main ones. On either side of the arch is a buttress with trefoil-headed niche and pedestal for an image, and above, within a recessed canopy, the bust of a small figure. There is a pilaster above each buttress, which was formerly capped by a large pinnacle. Above the porch is a parvise with shouldered, arched south window, and above in the gable a lily plant, with a lizard on one side and another animal on the other. At the north-east corner of the porch there is a turret, containing the steps leading up to the parvise. The whole forms a very charming creation. The same church has another beautiful little porch of the same style at the east side of the south transept. Above the outer arch is a triangular pediment enclosing a quatrefoil-shaped niche. Some of our cathedrals have noble porches of this period ; but these are beyond our ken, as we are only concerning ourselves with village churches. Very few timber porches were built in Early English times, but there is a notable example at Chevington, in Suffolk. The dog-tooth ornament appears on the beams of the old roof, and Time has spared its ancient timbers and added beauty to its appearance. Wooden porches became more general in the Decorated period of English architecture. A low wall of brick or stone was erected, and upon this the wooden framework placed. Stout, squared timbers formed the uprights ; the lower parts were panelled, and above them an open tracery window appears, formed after the fashion of the stone Decorated heads of windows of the period. Curved timbers, forming an arch, constitute the door, surmounted by a beam. The roof is massive, with curved braces, and has extended eaves in order to protect the woodwork from the weather. The gable projects some distance over the entrance, and has bargeboards with delightful curves and open tracery, which add much to the beauty of the structure. On each side of the porch are seats for the accommodation, not of idle visitors but for the persons who were waiting for the religious duties and ceremonies connected with the porch.

But these wooden porches were not the only ones erected during the fourteenth century in the Decorated style. There are many stone-built porches of this period, sometimes of large dimensions, with a room in the upper story. We usually call this upper chamber a parvise. I am aware that there are objections to this use of the word, which seems originally to have been applied to the *atrium*, or open space in front of a church, sometimes called the Paradise. For what purpose was the room constructed, and what were its uses? It often contains a fireplace, showing that it was inhabited. A spiral staircase of stone steps led to it from the church, sometimes set in the thickness of the wall or in a turret adjoining the porch or within the church itself. Many of these chambers contain a piscina, showing that there must have been an altar therein and that the Mass was celebrated there.

It is not easy to determine all the various uses to which this chamber was assigned or what was its original purpose. It has certainly been used as a treasury for the goods of the church. Frequently there is found a strong iron-bound chest for the keeping of the valuables of the church. Probably the clerk or sexton who guarded the relics preserved in the church resided in this room. When the church was served by some monastery the monk who officiated may have lived for a time there. Libraries were sometimes formed for the benefit of the parish priest and stored in the parvise. In quite small churches such libraries still exist, though, alas ! some of their most valuable treasures have disappeared, the collections of books being badly guarded and indifferently supervised. At the little village of Denchworth there is quite a good library, and among its treasures was Caxton's *Golden Legend,*

1483, which was sold by the vicar to an Oxford bookseller for £20 in 1853 and is now in the Bodleian Library. There still remain four volumes of Thomas Aquinas, dated 1485, and a copy of the fourth edition of Cranmer's Bible, 1541. Formerly the books were chained. These books are now in the vicarage, but they used to be placed in a room over the porch, built by one Gregory Geering, patron and churchwarden. There are libraries at Sutton Courtney, in Berkshire ; Finedon, in Northamptonshire ; Shipdam, in Norfolk, which has very early works ; and in many other churches.

The church was always considered to be the centre of the life of the village. Built of stone, it was a safer repository for the deeds and documents relating to private property than the thatched farms of the district. Hence these were often stored in the parvise, as well as the books containing the parochial accounts, the registers and church plate, and parish chests which held these priceless documents and treasure. Moreover, each parish was required to furnish fully equipped men-at-arms for the king's service, and among the miscellaneous collections contained in the parvise were helmets and breastplates and weapons of offence, which have remained long after the special need of them had passed away. At Broadwater Church, near Worthing, there is an old helmet which for a long time did duty as an almsbox.

G

At Horncastle we have seen a store of scythes fitted on to handles which, we believe, were used as primitive weapons in the Pilgrimage of Grace.

Another use of the parvise was that of a school. Indeed, some ingenious etymologist has erroneously suggested that the name is connected with *parvis*, a school for young folks. Before the days of compulsory education and palatial school-buildings this little chamber was found quite convenient for the purpose, and in a Gloucestershire church parvise I have seen the paintings on the wall made by an ingenious schoolmaster in order to teach historical events. If I remember rightly, there was a picture of an elephant charging, which may have illustrated the conquest of the Welsh tribes by the Romans in a battle fought on Gloucestershire soil.

In the fourteenth century many fine porches were built, and possess the characteristic features of the Decorated style. There is a profusion of the ball-flower ornament. Crocketed and gabled buttresses, with niches for statues, are on each side of the entrance, which is of several recessed orders. Above the arch is a niche for a statue, and the gable is crowned by an ornate cross. The roof is often vaulted or of timber, and the windows at the sides have the delicate tracery which prevailed in the fourteenth century.

A very large number of porches belong to the Perpendicular period, during which the masons often destroyed the work of their predecessors and erected more elaborate buildings. In Suffolk there is a village called Boxford, the church of which has a magnificent porch. There is no parvise, but it is lofty, with a large entrance door flanked by elaborately decorated buttresses and surmounted by stonework containing seven niches. There are carvings in the spandrels, an embattled parapet at the side, and two large windows, separated by a buttress on the east and west sides. Niches with canopies, panelled work decoration, and profuse ornamentation distinguish many examples of this style. Many timber porches were erected at this time, a very fine example of which exists at Ewelme, in Oxfordshire. Longcot Church, Berkshire, has a fifteenth-century porch, with well-moulded bargeboards, but somewhat mutilated, over the outer timber arch.

Although Herrick wrote a porch-verse, most of the ceremonies connected with the structure seem to have been discontinued after the Reformation, and the Book of Common Prayer does not recognize its existence. Some few porches, however, date from post-Reformation times and have Renaissance details. We may mention the porch at Ashurst, in Kent, which was built in 1621. It is of rough stonework, with a plain, unmoulded arch of the depressed form common in all late Tudor work, having in the gable a small, worn sundial, beneath which, under a label, and within a square recess, are the arms of Sir John Rivers, of Chafford. Chiddingstone porch is a good example of the combination of classic detail with the forms of the departing Gothic style. The arch is semicircular, with a keystone and capitals to the jambs, all moulded in the Renaissance style, but the whole is placed under a square-headed dripstone in the Perpendicular manner. The corbels under the springing of the gables are formed into classic trusses, and in the centre of the gable is a well-finished sundial, over which is carved the date 1626. Beneath the ivy, which should be removed, is a cross trefoiled at the extremities.[1] At Groombridge the porch shows no traces of Gothic influence. Some late porches are terrible structures in the debased style of " Churchwarden Gothic," which need not be particularized.

You will notice the benches or stone seats which occupy the interior sides of the porch. These were not intended merely for weary worshippers to rest upon after a long walk, but for the friends and relatives of those who were taking part in the ceremonies which formerly took place within the building. At Great Tew we have already seen two sets of seats, one higher than the other, the latter probably having been used by children.

Some peculiarities of particular porches may be

[1] These porches are described by Mr. Tavener-Perry in *The Memorials of Old Kent*, edited by myself and Mr. G. Clinch.

noted. At Broadwater, Sussex, there is a curious circular opening on the west of the north door about five feet from the ground. It has been suggested that through it a servitor would receive messages brought from persons who were dying and required the last sacrament, which messages the servitor would convey to one of the canons or monks in the monastery that stood on the site of the present manor house. I know not whether this be the true interpretation.

On the wall of the porch facing south you may often see a sundial. In the days before clocks were common the ordinary life of the village would be governed by the time recorded by this sundial. The oldest belong to the Saxon period. There is one at Old Byland, now preserved in the tower ; it is semicircular and is engraved on a flat stone. It bears the inscription :—

+ SVMARLETHAN HVSCARL ME FECIT.

Kirkdale has a noted Saxon sundial, which my friend Dr. Fryer thus describes [1] : " It consists of a flat stone about seven feet wide and two feet high. It is divided into three compartments, the centre one being devoted to the dial and the outer ones to the inscription. The dial is a semicircle, standing on its curved side. The gnomon (long disappeared) stood out from the centre, and from the socket radii extended so as to divide the day

[1] *Antiquary*, iv. p. 136.

into eight portions, the five greater lines marking the centre of each ' tide ' being terminated by crosses. Every letter of the following inscription may be read to-day :—

+ ORM . GAMALSVNA BOHTE . SCS . GREGORIVS . MINSTER
THINNE . HIT . WÆS . AL . TOBROCAN . AND . TOFALLAN . AND .
HE . HIT . LET . MACAN . NEWAN . FROM . GRVNDE . CHRE .
AND . SCS . GREGORIVS . IN . EADWARD . DAGVM . CNC . AND .
IN . TOSTI . DAGUM . EORL .

Engraved round and beneath the dial are the words :—

+ THIS . IS . DÆGES . SOLMORCA . ÆT ILCVM . TIDE
+ AND . HAWARD . ME . WROHTE . AND . BRAND . PRS.

This has been translated : ' Orm Gamal's son bought St. Gregory's Minster, when it was all broken and fallen. He let it be made new from the ground, to Christ and St. Gregory, in Edward's days—the King ; in Tosti's days—the earl. This is the day's sun-maker at every season ; and Hawarth wrought me and Brand the priest.' "

History tells us much about this Gamal, who tried to play a double game in the dangerous days before the Conqueror came, and was murdered by Earl Tosti.

On the famous Bewcastle Cross there is a dial, and another at Edston, inscribed :—

HOROLOGIVM | VIATORVM—LOTHAN ME WROTHEA.

There are the remains of Saxon dials at Bishopstone, near Newhaven, Weaverthorpe, Headbourne Worthy, Barnack, and Swillington.

In subsequent periods sundials continued to be affixed to the porches and towers of churches, and sometimes to tombstones, as at Clifford, in Herefordshire, where an inscription thus moralizes :—

> Learn from the shadow on the dial
>   How quick our hours onward move ;
> Be mindful in this state of tryal
>   Every moment to improve.

Our forefathers were very fond of attributing to the dial the voice of the preacher. Thus, at Linstead Church, Kent, we find the lines :—

> Every moment well improved
> Secures an age in heaven.

They were also very fond of a little witticism. Occasionally they perpetrated the following little joke. They place at the top of the dial the words WE MUST, or WE SHALL, the dial itself completing the sentence, which thus reads, " We must dial —*i.e.* die all." This appears at Kedleston, Derbyshire, Buxted, Sussex, and Bromsgrove, Worcestershire. Bradbury's sundial, in Cheshire, bids us " Work while it is day," and Ellastone's warns us to " Watch and pray—Time flies." Cornish sundials tell the obvious truth, " Every hour shortens life " (St. Austell) ; " *una umbra et vapor est hominum vita* " (Helston) ; and a porch-dial at Tavistock states " *hora pars vitæ*."

With such sentiments did our sires adorn their sundials, which were honoured long after the church clock marked the hours with its single hand or took to itself two hands and took cognizance of the fleeting minutes. We should like to have told its story too, and to try to describe the quaint astronomical clocks, such as that at Wimborne Minster and Ottery St. Mary's, and the quarter-jacks and armoured figures which perform prodigies of valour whenever the clock strikes the hour, though these are rare and are seldom found in village churches. But the clock reminds us that time flies, and that it is impossible in a single volume to describe everything that a church contains.

We must, however, mention one dial which is unique. It is placed in the interior of the church at Dartford, on the inner splay of the sill of the south-east window, and bears the names of the vicar and churchwardens who were in office in 1820. In spite of its unfavourable position, it contrives to record the time when the sun shines during the afternoon. It is believed that there is no other sundial that marks the hours in the interior of a church.

CHAPTER VII

DOORS AND DOORWAYS

IN all ages of Gothic architecture from Norman times onwards the builders of our churches have striven to invest the entrances to the Houses of God with distinction and special adornment. They seem to have concentrated their imagination, their art, and skill in masonry in investing their doorways with all that they could devise to make them beautiful and worthy of Him whom they worshipped within the sanctuary. All their wealth of imagery was showered down upon them. By the presentment of scriptural subjects, of the Divine Head of the Church, of type and figure, of symbolism which in these days it is difficult to interpret, they endeavoured to impress the minds and hearts of those who were entering the sacred buildings in order that the worshippers might pay their homage to the Most High with true reverence and in a right spirit.

They seem to have taken for their guidance the words of our Lord, who said, " I am the Door ; by Me if any man enter in he shall be saved " ; and to have resolved to make the entrance to

His house as fair and beautiful as the art and skill of man could accomplish. Sometimes during the Early English period the door is made double, which is meant to signify our Lord's two natures, human and divine ; and the three doors at the west end of large churches typify the Blessed Trinity.

In the doorways fashioned in Anglo-Saxon times we see no such effort. We notice them at Bradford-on-Avon, in Aldhelm's charming church there, and in many other buildings of the period, plain, round-headed entrances with square-edged jambs, the openings being simple, cut square through the walls without any orders or recessed divisions as in the later styles. As I have stated in another book : [1]—

The stone-work of the arch is plain, and a hood or arch of rib-work projecting from the surface of the wall surrounds the doorway, and is continued down to the ground. . . . The arch rests upon a rude and frequently plain block capital, termed an impost.

An attempt is sometimes made to decorate these imposts by bands of masonry standing out in relief and by the projection of the upper and lower parts.

Some Saxon doorways have triangular heads, and are formed simply by placing two blocks of stone so as to form two sides of an isosceles triangle, the lower ends resting upon the imposts.

[1] *Handbook to English Gothic Architecture* (Dent & Sons).

In all this you will perceive that there is very little attempt at making the doorway impressive or decorative. But all this was altered when the Normans began to rear their massive churches. At first they were content to make their doorways plain and strong, with little ornamentation save bold roll mouldings and shallow adornments. But when the first thirty years of the twelfth century had passed away their doorways blossomed out into a wonderful variety of enrichments. Doubtless the Norman ecclesiastics, who came over with the Conqueror, were responsible for some attempts at decoration, and a more enriched form of Romanesque than had previously been tried ; but it was more than sixty years after the Norman Conquest that these elaborate doorways began to be built, and owed their origin to a new and native school of true English art, which produced sculpture vastly different from that which manifested itself in France at the same period.

We will look more carefully at an example of a typical Norman doorway, and take as an instance that of Lullington, in Somerset. It will be observed that it is recessed, that is to say, the sides and head recede from the outward face of the wall, forming, as it were, steps, set horizontally. In the angles of each of these recesses small pillars or shafts are set with bases and capitals, and from the latter rise the round-headed arches adorned with Norman mouldings of different patterns. These arches fill the recesses in the head of the doorway corresponding with those at the sides. Each recess is called an Order. In this Lullington example there are only two Orders, but in more elaborate doorways there are several, which add dignity and beauty to the design.

Looking again at this Lullington doorway we notice that immediately above the door and beneath the arch there is a flat stone that has been sculptured. This is called a tympanum, and the carvings shown upon it are full of interest and repay careful study. There is a very large number of these tympana in various parts of the country, and a friend of the writer, Mr. Charles E. Keyser, F.S.A., has made a very close examination of almost every example in England, and thrown much light upon the curious subjects represented upon them.

On the Lullington tympanum there is the representation of a tree with two creatures, one on each side of it, devouring the tree. What is the meaning of this curious conception? It is one of the symbolical forms intended to enforce the truths of the Christian religion. The tree represents the Tree of Spiritual Life and Knowledge, and the skilful and pious sculptor wished to impress upon the minds of all who were about to worship in the sacred building, the claim of the Church to be the source whence all spiritual sustenance could be obtained by those who were really eager to

NORMAN DOORWAY, LULLINGTON CHURCH, SOMERSET

receive it.   That this is the correct interpretation of the symbol of the Tree is proved by an inscription upon the lintel of a doorway at Dinton, placed beneath a similar representation of a tree with animals devouring it.   The inscription is as follows, and will at first perhaps puzzle the reader :—

+ Premiapromeritissiyisdcsperethabenda
Audiathicprseptasibiquesitretinenda +

When properly set out the Latin runs as follows :—

Præmia pro meritis si quis desperet habenda
Audiat hic præcepta sibi quæ sint retinenda,

and may be translated, " If any one shall despair of obtaining reward for his deserts, let him attend to the doctrines here preached, and take care to keep them in mind." The animals represented at Lullington are a lion on the right and a griffin on the left.   Possibly the idea of the influences of good and evil may be intended to be introduced.

Another subject is a man with griffins on each side, and seems to illustrate Psalm xliv, verses 18-20 : " When Thou hast smitten us into the place of dragons," etc.   Other favourite subjects are : a figure of our Lord, in allusion to His saying " I am the Door," the Agnus Dei, Adam and Eve, a simple cross, St. Michael fighting with Satan, represented as an immense dragon with terrible jaws and extended tongue, and our Lord in majesty. This last figure is shown in the illustration of Lullington, where it appears in a niche above the doorway.

The figure of St. George appears occasionally on Norman tympana, though he was not adopted as the Patron Saint of England until a later time. At Fordington there is the unique representation of the saint as the champion of Christendom. The stonework is irregular, and made to fit the octagonal-headed doorway, and on it is carved St. George on horseback holding a long spear with a pennon at one end, and the other pressed into the mouth of a prostrate soldier, who is grasping it in his hand as he is being hurled down. Two others lie dead before him, and on the left are two more kneeling with upraised hands. Mr. Keyser says of this that we have a representation of the miraculous intervention of the saint in the battle between the Christians and Saracens before the walls of Antioch.

It is difficult sometimes to interpret the meaning of some of these strange carvings. At Hognaston there is the quaint figure of a man holding a pastoral staff and of various animals. That on the right is evidently the Agnus Dei bearing a cross, and above the figure are two birds. The central figure represents a bishop with his pastoral staff in his right hand and a book in his left pressed to his breast. He is, doubtless, conducting various animals to do homage to the Lamb of God. At

Parwich there is a somewhat similar subject. There is the Agnus Dei with a dove on its head, and the animals are coming to do homage to it. First comes a stag, a noble animal, who is helping the Lamb to trample down snakes, representing vice. Then comes a lion, the king of beasts, who is having some trouble with his trefoiled tail, and then there is a pig, an unworthy, unclean beast, who is retreating from the Lamb. Here we have some idea of the forces of vice opposed to the practice of a virtuous and moral life.

We must refer once more to the doorway at Lullington. You will notice the moulding round the arch. It is composed of a series of heads of birds with long beaks, and is called the beak-head moulding. This refers to the birds of the air in the Parable of the Sower, ever ready to dart down upon the careless and indifferent hearers of God's Word, and to snatch away the seed that has been sown in their hearts. The other moulding in the lower arch is called a zigzag. Many other mouldings were used by these Norman builders, such as the alternate billet, double cone, cable, embattled, lozenge, pellet, star, nail-head, indented ; and it is always possible to discover each style of Gothic architecture by the peculiarities of the mouldings.

When the Early English style asserted itself the exuberant fancy of the Norman masons was not so evident. The pointed arch was, of course, generally used, and on each side of the doorway there were one or more detached shafts with capitals adorned with sculptured stiff-leaved foliage. The mouldings of the arches in use during this period are the bowtell, roll and fillet, rounds and hollows, and the dog-tooth ornament is characteristic of the style. In some of the larger village churches we find the doorway divided into two arches by a slender shaft, a larger arch enfolding the lesser ones. In the centre of the head of the larger arch there appears some sculptured foliage or a quatre-foil opening. The head of the smaller doorways is often trefoiled.

In the fourteenth century the capitals of the shafts on each side usually disappear and the mouldings of the arch are continued down the sides. When there are shafts, as in the preceding style, they do not stand away from the walled recess, but form parts of the arch mouldings. The favourite mouldings are the scroll, curve and slant, sunk quarter round, sunk chamfer, wave, ogee, and the ball-flower and the four-leaved flower are the usual ornaments. The capitals have clusters of foliage, like a ball of flowers. These doorways are highly decorated. The dripstone is often sup-ported by carved heads ; niches and canopies orna-mented with crockets and finials are placed above the door, and a figure of our Lord, or the Virgin, or some saint, appears therein, if vandalism and Puritan iconoclasm have suffered it to remain.

The Perpendicular doorways have a heavy, square-headed hood-moulding, with a curious angular return at its lowest point. The arch is Tudor shaped, and small shafts with plain capitals octagonal in shape are on each side. The usual ornaments are the rose and the Tudor flower, and the favourite mouldings are the wave, ogee and cavetto, bowtell, and double ogee. The favourite panel-work of the Perpendicular buildings or heraldic shields appear in the spandrels.

In many village churches the original doors remain, some dating back to Norman times—stout, sturdy oaken timbers, strengthened with iron, that could well resist the attacks of robber bands and northern pirates, for which purpose they were often sorely needed. These Norman doors are remarkable for their strong ornamented hinges. These were formed of a triple strap, one extending across the door, and the others curved round in the form of the letter C, or, as Mr. Starkie Gardner describes them, " like the horns of a crescent." He suggests that this triple form may have been regarded as symbolic, and points out that as the springing of these straps was behind the stonework of the doorway, it was more difficult to wrench them off. The ends of these straps were beaten into scrolls or foliage or heads of serpents. There are usually two or three hinges to each door, and there were additional bars and straps which made it very strong. Moreover, we sometimes find weird

H

iron figures fastened to the door, such as at Stillingfleet, in Yorkshire, where a Vikings' ship appears, and some other objects which it is difficult to recognize. At Staplehurst, Kent, there is a Vikings' ship, and also fishes, goose, sea-dragon, snakes, and crosses, a strange collection. Perhaps the makers intended to ward off evil by these signs, just as modern folk fasten horseshoes to their doors.

There are remarkable Norman doors at Hormead and at Willingale Spain, near Ongar, Essex. An immense variety is shown in this ironwork. We have an interesting form in our county of Berkshire on the north door of the church at Sparsholt, near Wantage. In this case the ironwork may be older than the door, and, as was not unusual, may have been taken off an older door when the wood became decayed and fastened on the present one.

In the thirteenth century, when the fear of roving bands of marauders was less, the doors became less defensive, and the scroll-work became more elaborate. The smith found opportunity for his skill in the beautiful grilles that adorn some of our cathedrals, and fashioned charming foliated scrollwork, as on the doors of Worksop Priory and Market Deeping. The C or crescent-shaped hinges continue, but these are adorned with scrollwork and vine leaves. In our Berkshire churches of Faringdon and Uffington there still remain examples of this Early English work. The discovery of using stamps produced a wonderful effect on the art of smithing, and enabled the artist to accomplish more intricate designs. Later on the art of the smith who worked with forge and hammer and anvil died, and the ironworker began to treat the metal when it was cold, using file and saw, vice and drill, bolting or riveting the pieces together without heat, or tenoning and morticing them as a carpenter would treat wood. The hinges of the fourteenth and fifteenth century lack the elaborate character of the earlier examples, but still occasionally spread their scrolls over the door. In several cases each scroll ends in a fleur-de-lis. There is a fine example at Great Casterton.

The smiths devoted much skill to the fashioning of door-handles and locks and keys, and sometimes of knockers. People are accustomed to call them sanctuary knockers, and instance that at Durham Cathedral, which was certainly used by the poor creatures who, escaping from their pursuers, sought safety and claimed the privilege of sanctuary within the precincts of St. Cuthbert's shrine.

There are not many left in England, but besides at Durham, others may be found at All Saints, Pavement, York, Adel, in Yorkshire, and St. Gregory's, Norwich. In all these examples they are " large bronze escutcheons representing the head of a gruesome monster with locks flowing and jaws extended, and in some cases the head of a man within them. Through the monster's mouth hangs a massive ring, which in days gone by served as the Hagody or sanctuary knocker, at which when ' offenders did come and knocke, streightwaie they were letten in at any time of the nyght.' "

But every church was a sanctuary, though this was sometimes violated, and not a very secure harbourage, as fugitives from justice needed food, which could not always be found in a village church. There is a very curious knocker on the door of the church of St. Nicholas, Gloucester, admirably fashioned, and though it does not belong to a country church, I may be allowed to describe it here. In the centre is a large sinister-looking demon with long flowing hair and ears, bat-shaped wings and hairy forelegs with sharp claws. He holds a large ring in his mouth, and has on his back the head of an old woman, with her face looking upwards, and her extended tongue licking a bunch of grapes hanging above her. Evidently it is intended as a warning against drunkenness, and to show the punishment that awaited the confirmed inebriate, who is endeavouring to imbibe a final taste of the juice of the grape which has been her ruin.[1]   The knocker is attached to a

---

[1] A spirited illustration of this is given in the *Journal of the British Archæological Association*, with a description by Mr. C. E. Keyser, F.S.A., from which the above is taken.

hexagonal plate that is fastened to the door by cone-shaped headed nails. The figure is made of bronze and is probably of fourteenth-century date.

If we examine the shafts on each side of the doorway, or the adjacent walls, we find a number of little crosses rudely carved with a knife or chisel, and people often wonder why they were cut there. Some ignorant folk have actually called them consecration crosses, which, as we have seen, were something very different. These are votive crosses, and were cut by some person who, when he was about to start on a journey or pilgrimage, which in mediaeval times was attended with some danger, would thus register a vow that, if God would keep him safe, he would make some thank-offering on his return for the Divine mercy and blessing. These little crosses are witnesses of the simple faith of our mediaeval forefathers, and of the age when religion and life were bound together by the closest of ties.

Some doors show signs of a gruesome covering, and are said to have the skins of Danish marauders nailed to them. Dean Hole was once asked whether he had discovered any traces on the doors of Rochester Cathedral, and replied that he was too busy to trouble himself about the epidermis of a Dane ; but he was told that as the custodian of a church he ought to take at least as much interest in its history as in the cultivation of roses.

At Copford and Hadstock, in Essex, there are doors covered with human skins, and also at Westminster and Worcester Cathedral.

Having sufficiently, I trust, examined the door and doorway, we will now enter the church and try to discover its many treasures.

CHAPTER VIII

THE INTERIOR OF THE CHURCH

ON passing through the doorway into the church we notice first, close to the door—sometimes it is just outside the church in the porch—the remains of a holy water stoup, which frequently was attached to the first pier on the right hand close to the entrance. In Roman Catholic churches the stoup is still in use, and it seems a pity that it was discarded at the Reformation, since it teaches a useful lesson, and symbolizes the purity of heart and mind which should characterize those who enter the sanctuary of God. There may have been some abuses connected with the use of holy water in mediaeval times, but these need not have deprived the English Church of the reverent use. The fact that so many of these stoups are damaged shows the hostility with which their contents was regarded by the extreme Reforming party. Many of them are quite unadorned ; but there are several examples of stoups with a niche over them. Norman stoups often consist of a stone shaft adorned with characteristic mouldings and having a cushion capital, which is hollowed out so as to form the receptacle for holy water. Canopied stoups are not uncommon. In *English Church Furniture* Dr. Cox enumerates many examples of stoups that remain in our churches, including the very beautiful one at Harlton St. Mary, Cambridgeshire, which is supported on three detached shafts and has a shell-like basin, and also a remarkable heraldic example at Endellion, Cornwall, which was placed there by one John Roscarrock about the year 1500. Sometimes, as at Lastingham, they assume the size of a small font. Churchwardens' accounts sometimes refer to the erection of these stoups. Nor did their use entirely disappear at the Reformation. As late as 1548-9 we find one being erected at Hawkhurst church, where there appears in the church books, "Item for a holly water stop of stone of George Afford xiid."

Not far from the door stands the font, which will be described in a separate chapter, and in order to encourage the charity of the faithful when they are leaving the church an almsbox usually is placed near the entrance. It is commonly made of wood and iron and is fastened by an iron band to the wall or pillar. Few pre-Reformation boxes remain. There is a very fine one at Blythburgh, Suffolk, and others are enumerated in the book on Church Furniture in the *Antiquary's Books*. Later examples often bear the inscription, "Remember the Poor," the last word being spelt in divers fashions. There is a quaint little almsbox at Watton, Norfolk, which assumes the form of a beggar soliciting alms and bearing on his breast the above-mentioned advice, with the date 1639.

Passing onwards, we find ourselves in the nave of the church, which takes its name from the Latin *navis* and the Saxon *nafa* or *nafu*, and is so called as representing the ark or ship of the Church, in which those who seek salvation may take refuge and sail over " the waves and through the storms of this troublesome world until they reach the haven where they would be." It is the chief part or body of the church, extending from the west end to the chancel screen or to that constructional division marking off the part occupied by the faithful from that in which divine service is sung and the holy mysteries celebrated. From this point we can take a general survey of the church, the principal details of which we will admire later on.

We are imagining ourselves in a church with aisles. There is an arcade on either side of us, the piers and arches of which are not all of the same date. Those in the centre are evidently Norman. The pillars are low and massive, and support heavy round-headed arches. They are cylindrical, as is usual in country churches, but in some we find them shaped square or octagonal, and, as I have pointed out elsewhere,[1] are adorned with a spiral fluting. There are often sub-arches re-

---

[1] *English Gothic Architecture* (Dent), p. 52.

cessed within the outer arch. The capitals of the piers are what are called cushion, or scallop, or volute, and the bases are circular, standing on a square plinth.

The chancel was not all finished at one time, as we notice the two western arches are different from the Norman ones. The arch is pointed ; the piers are formed of columns surrounded by detached shafts, united upon one base and under one capital, and bound together by a band half-way up. The capitals are bell-shaped and covered with sculptured foliage of the stiff-leaved character, and the dog-tooth ornament appears on the arches, with mouldings characteristic of the style. Owing to the fall of the tower in the fourteenth century the two arches and piers at the east end of the nave were destroyed, and had to be rebuilt in the style then in vogue. This is called Decorated. The piers are composed of columns which are no longer detached, as in those at the west end, but closely joined together, and in some cases we have plain cylindrical or octagonal piers. The sculpture upon the capital imitates nature more closely than that on the Early English examples, and the ball-flower is the usual ornament and hall-mark of Decorated work. Evidently some alteration or restoration was found necessary in the fifteenth century, as in our typical church two of the piers have been rebuilt. They are unlike the others. They are thinner. There are no capitals, as the mouldings are carried up in a continuous sweep to the head of the arch, which is no longer pointed, but four-centred. You are sure to find some panelling either in the spandrels, or on the surface of the sub-arch, or on the wall above the arch. Perpendicular capitals are adorned with plain rings and the bases are often octagonal with a chamfered top, surmounted by a smaller octagonal piece and then by a sort of inverted capital.

Many country churches have no clerestory, but we may suppose our typical church to have one. It contains a series of windows formed of quatrefoil or trefoil openings, or of lancets or three or four lights under one head. On either side of the arcade are aisles, and perhaps a chantry chapel has been built out on the south side. We see a glorious screen that extends across the church from aisle wall to aisle wall, about which we shall have something to say presently. On the left hand is a marvellous pulpit, which will be hereafter described, and on the left an old-fashioned lectern.

The western tower opens into the nave, and a fine large window sheds light into the west end and looks glorious during the evening service in summer, when the rays of the setting sun shine resplendent through the old stained glass, lighting them with a thousand colourings. In olden days the church was a blaze of colour. Walls, tombs, altars, images, were all painted, even the stone carvings on capitals ; and the church had not that bare look which now too often characterizes our ecclesiastical edifices. They suffered also during the age of whitewash, when our forefathers covered everything with a white coating, which did one service, as it helped to preserve much that otherwise would have become decayed.

This particular church of ours is very large for a country village. You could seat all the parishioners in a quarter of the nave, even if every man, woman, and child came to the services, which they certainly do not. Why was it built so large? It may be that, in mediaeval times, in the days of the prosperity of the wool trade, the population was much larger than it is now, when rural industries have decayed and manufacturers have all congregated where coal abounds and steam can be raised. But that is not all the explanation. Our forefathers built their churches not merely for the seating of a congregation, as we do in this degenerate age. They built them for the honour and glory of Him whom they worshipped, and no fane was deemed too large or too fine for that exalted purpose. Moreover, every parishioner paid over to the church a tithe, or one-tenth, of all his possessions, either in goods, or work, or money. He did not grumble at this, as people did in the old days of Church Rates ; but it appears that there was a kind of holy rivalry to see who could do the most to enrich and beautify God's House.

The men, if they were craftsmen, gave their time, while the women kept the church well supplied with embroidery, from copes and altar frontals, heavy with needlework and jewelry, to fair linens and purificators.

Our typical church, then, being much too large for the village, possesses two transepts, besides a noble chancel, which is separated from the nave by a fine screen. The choir, since the time of the early Christian basilicas, has been separated from the nave by low screen walls, called *cancelli*, whence we derive our word chancel. This particular church has a long, large chancel, and the reason of this is that there was a monastic cell in the village attached to a distant monastery, and monks lived here in the ruined buildings on the other side of the road, and used the chancel of this church for their daily services. Therein they chanted their services of the Seven Hours, and in the chancel there are misericords, which we shall examine more carefully presently, or seats of pity, to enable them to withstand the fatigue of their lengthy devotions.

In large churches there is not only the nave arcade and the clerestory, but between them the triforium arcade, and behind it a gallery between the roof and vaulting of the aisles ; but few village churches can boast of this dignified structure, and I need not describe it at any length. We look up and admire the old roof with its beams and king-post, or queen-posts, hammer-beams, curved braces, and purlins. It is probably not the original roof, as time and weather caused its decay, and as we have seen, when we examined the exterior of the church, it was more highly pitched than the present one, which was erected in the fourteenth or fifteenth century and is much finer than its predecessor. There is a series of tie-beams stretching across the church, their ends resting on upright timbers supported on corbels. Beneath these beams are curved braces, one end of each brace fastened to the wall, while the other end extends to the centre of the beam and then meets the other brace, thus forming an arch. Above the centre of the beam is a post placed perpendicular to it and extending to the apex of the roof, supporting the great cross-beam that runs east and west and forms the apex. This is called a king-post. Sometimes instead of a king-post there are two queen-posts, which rise from the tie-beam at a distance of about one-third of its length from each wall, and have a cross-piece running parallel with the tie-beam joining the top of the posts where they meet the slanting beams that support the roof. The vacant spaces between the tie-beams and braces are often occupied by pierced panels. The sloping part of the roof is divided into squares by pieces of timber called purlins, which are adorned with mouldings and bosses at their intersection. Some roofs are constructed on the principle of a hammer-beam arrangement. That is to say, the tie-beams do not extend across the church, but extend a short distance into the church, and are supported by curved braces as before. From the ends of these queen-posts arise with a cross-piece as before, from the centre of which a king-post with supporting timbers rises to the apex. Sometimes curved timbers rise from the ends of the hammer-beams to the apex.

In East Anglia there are many fine timber roofs, and a famous example is that of the church of Willingham, Cambridgeshire. It belongs to the Perpendicular period, and is of the hammer-beam type. It has thirteen compartments and twice as many hammer-beams. At the end of each hammer-beam is a carved angel with expanded wings. The spandrels are filled with pierced tracery. The pitch of the roof is very high for a roof of this period. All the timbers are elaborately moulded, and the cornice is fringed with ornament.[1] It is said that this roof was brought here from Barnwell Abbey, near Cambridge, but upon this question authorities differ. But all the roofs are not of timber construction. The aisles may be vaulted in stone, and it is not difficult to find examples of the various modes of vaulting, and to trace its history from the plain barrel vault of the Norman style to the lierne or tracery vaulting of the Decorated period, until we

[1] *Churches of Cambridgeshire*, by C. H. Evelyn-White, F.S.A.

arrive at the complicated network of ribs and the fan tracery with pendants of the fifteenth and sixteenth century.[1] The bosses should be especially noted. Upon them are carved such subjects as heads of ecclesiastics, the five wounds of Christ, angels, the Dove, heraldic achievements, rebuses, grotesques, etc.

There are some curious openings on either side of the chancel arch. They are unglazed. What is their object? "Oh, those are lepers' windows," I have heard people confidently affirm, being ignorant that lepers were never allowed within a church. Of course, their proper name is " squints "—some persons persist in calling them " hagioscopes," a Greek word for an entirely English object. The old English word is better, though it is sometimes applied to people's defective vision. The object of a squint was to enable that portion of the congregation assembled in the transept to see the elevation of the Host in the service of the Mass.

Our church is provided with pews, most of them being deal or pitch-pine seats, which look very new and out of place in this ancient building. There are, however, some stone seats running along the side of the walls of the nave, where the aged and

---

[1] I have described these various kinds of vaulting in my *Handbook of Gothic Architecture.* It is too large a subject to be entered upon in this book, and the reader will find full descriptions of vaultings in Mr. Francis Bond's new book, and in *A History of Architectural Development,* by F. M. Simpson.

infirm could sit during service-time.   The rest of the congregation used to stand or kneel.   This is the origin of the saying, " Let the weakest go to the wall."   In mediaeval times, although there were more sermons preached than is generally supposed, preaching was not considered an essential part of the service, and seats were not therefore so requisite as they are now, or when the Carolean divines used to " hold-forth " for an hour or more, and were not even restrained by the running out of the hour-glass.   Many churches retain their stone seats, which must have been a boon and a blessing to the old people in the days when no better seating accommodation was provided.   Preaching became more common in the fifteenth and sixteenth centuries, hence it was found necessary to provide benches for the use of the hearers.   They were low, open seats, made of oak, sometimes carved at the back and panelled, with the ends higher than the rest.   These ends gave an opportunity for the exercise of the wood-carver's art, who sometimes produced strange and weird designs and raised the heads, carving them into what are called poppy-heads.   There are some plain benches at Tysoe Church and at Wootton Wawen, Warwickshire, and some backless examples at Cawston, Norfolk, which have finely carved poppy-heads. The carvings on the ends are much varied.   Rich men often left money in their wills for the *puying* of churches, and recorded their benefactions by

I

placing their coat-of-arms. Thus, at Colebrooke Church, Devonshire, the bench ends bear the arms of Coplestone, one John Coplestone having been the founder in the fifteenth century. At Sutcombe, in the same county, there appear on the bench ends the arms of the Prideaux family ; and heraldic devices with the initials of the person who gave the seats can be found in many churches.

There still exists a very interesting account of the re-seating of Chesham Church, Bucks, in 1606, the necessity of which arose from the increase of the population, and because " many had seated themselves as they thought fit, and some of the meanest account had gotten the best seats and would sit with persons of far better reckoning, many also challenging places in one seat, and so sat in heaps without any respect of decency or order." Some of the parishioners objected to the scheme and refused to pay the rate, one of whom was arrested, and then paid. There was much going to and fro between Chesham and Lambeth, and sundry charges for " horsemeat and bote hire," but the whole matter was carried through at length, including the repair of the bells and the erection of a gallery. We are glad to see the record that the first seat in the middle cross alley was reserved for six " ancient men that cannot hear well." [1]

[1] *Antiquary*, vol. xxxv. p. 19. A paper by Rev. C. H. Evelyn-White, F.S.A.

In the book *English Church Furniture* Dr. Cox and Mr. Alfred Harvey have recorded a vast number of existing examples of these early church seats, and to this exhaustive work the reader is referred. The ends of many of them have strange carvings. At Brent Knoll, Somerset, there are some carvings of the adventures of Reynard the Fox, in one of which there is a very realistic representation of Reynard being hanged by geese. Fish, mermen and mermaids, beasts and dragons, angels, symbols of the Passion, including the crown of thorns, the nails and hammer, the reed and spear, the vesture, dice, the ladder, pierced hands and feet, and the cock that proclaimed the denial of St. Peter, are frequently carved, and also the sacred monogram and the crowned M for the Virgin Mary. At Blythburgh, Suffolk, there are carvings of the seven deadly sins and the four seasons. The word " poppy-head " has no relation to the flower ; it is derived from *puppis*, the stern of a ship. Balderton, Notts, has a large number of these adornments, which are made to represent rabbits with their heads downwards. At Combe-in-Teignhead there are some finely carved bench-ends showing figures of SS. Katherine, Barbara, and others.

It was not until the beginning of the seventeenth century that the fashion of erecting high pews and assigning them to important members of the con-gregation set in. These were frequently the objects of satire and censure by the authorities. The writers of the book to which I have just referred state that the squire's pew was the successor of the old chantry parclose, and that when the chantry was abolished at the Reformation, the lord of the manor retained possession of its site and erected his pew upon it. Imitating his example, the smaller gentry and farmers acquired, doubtless by paying some fees to the vicar, space for their pews or boxes, wherein, as an old Berkshire dame said, "they could sleep comfortable without all the parish knowin' on it." You will remember the story of Bishop Wilberforce, who was shown by the clerk the squire's pew, and when asked if he could suggest any additional convenience, proposed a card-table ! His scorn in the nineteenth century was somewhat similar to that of Bishop Corbett in the seventeenth, who thus inveighed against pews :—

"Stately pews are now become tabernacles with rings and curtains to them. There wants nothing but beds to hear the word of God on ; we have casements, locks, and keys, and cushions—I had almost said bolsters and pillows—and for these we love the Church. I will not guess what is done within them, who sits, stands, or lies asleep at prayers, communion, etc., but this I dare say, they are either to hide some vice, or to proclaim one ; to hide disorder or to proclaim pride."

The squire's pew in many churches, before the

days of " restoration," was a very cosy, sleep-pro-
voking structure, curtained off, wherein was often
a special fireplace, the pew being furnished with
armchairs like a drawing-room. If the clergyman
was rather too long in preaching, the squire would
poke the fire somewhat impatiently and vigor-
ously. It is reported that sherry and biscuits were
sometimes served by a livery servant, and that the
squire used to have his letters and newspapers
delivered to him in his pew and to read them
during the sermon. At Felbrugg, Norfolk, the
home of the Windhams, the pew was large enough
to seat fourteen persons. It stood just west of
the chancel screen. There was a similar pew on
the opposite side of the central passage for the
rector's family.

Some of these pews are roofed in with carved
canopies, resembling somewhat the four-posted
bedsteads in which our forefathers loved to repose.
In my book on the *Parish Clerk* I quoted Dean
Swift's satire on them in *Baucis and Philemon* :—

> A bedstead of the antique mode,
> Compact of timber many a load,
> Such as our ancestors did use,
> Was metamorphosed into pews ;
> Which still their ancient nature keep
> By lodging folks disposed to sleep.

Some of these Jacobean canopied pews display
excellent wood-carving. In the days of my youth
I remember well the curious examples at Whalley,

in Lancashire, which have a close resemblance to four-posted beds ; but the carving is very fine and is believed to be the relic of an old chantry parclose work. A wonderful pew of Jacobean design exists at Stokesay, Salop. There is the noted " Spring pew " in Lavenham Church, Suffolk, with carved screens, recently restored. It takes its name from Thomas Spring, a wealthy clothier, who rebuilt the church, and therein ordered his executors to erect a parclose, or enclosure, before the altar of St. Katherine, for a chantry above his tomb, and his widow ordered in her will that a good honest priest should be engaged to perform the offices. This explains the origin of many of these enclosed pews, which were originally par-closed chantries.

When officiating in old churches wherein these old pews remain, such as North Crawley, in Buckinghamshire, I have noticed a curious effect when the congregation kneels in prayer. Every head disappears and one feels alone in the church. The hand of the restorer has fallen heavily on these old pews, which were condemned as irreverent boxes and unsuitable for a church. So the old oak structures were removed, and some church furniture makers have supplied brand new deal seats instead. I remember some fine old panelled pews from a northern church reposing for some years in the vicarage stables, and ultimately finding their way to wainscot an archdeacon's dining-room. We were rather sorry to note the recent restoration of the last Berkshire church containing the old-fashioned square pews, which have been ruthlessly removed from the place they have so long occupied.

Associated with these old pews and "three-decker" pulpits were the galleries that sometimes ran round the church in tiers like those in a theatre. In the eighteenth century and early nineteenth, people were very proud of their galleries, cheap wooden erections, which not only stood at the west end, but extended to the north and south sides. Happily our typical church has no such monstrosity. But it would be a mistake to condemn all western galleries, some of which are ancient and interesting. There is a fine singers' gallery at Puddletown, Dorset, immortalized by Thomas Hardy in *Far from the Madding Crowd*, and bearing the date 1635 on the finely carved oak front. The gallery extends across the north aisle, which part has an inscription HUC ADES NON VIDERI SED AUDIRE ET PRECARI. Another gallery is at Worstead, in Norfolk, bearing the date 1501, and another at Cawston in the same county. It bears the inscription, "God spede the plow," and was probably erected by the ploughmen's guild. Again turning to the east we look at the altar, the sedilia, reredos, piscina, credence, aumbreys, the memorials of squires and rectors, the fine brasses on the floor within the sanctuary, and in the vestry find much to interest us in the registers and other parish books, the church plate and other treasures which time and vandalism have spared. There is so much to see in an old church that the days are never long enough for their complete exploration.

CHAPTER IX

FONTS AND THEIR COVERS

THE baptismal fonts of England present many features of great interest and importance. They are remarkable for the beauty and the variety of their design, their architectural merits, and their great antiquity, surpassing in number and exquisite detail those of any other country. Nowhere on the Continent will you find such a remarkable series of ancient and interesting fonts as in the British Isles.

In the middle of the eleventh century Pope Leo IV ordered the clergy to provide fonts in churches.[1] Previous to that period they were rare, but not unknown. There is the very interesting example at Deerhurst, Gloucestershire, the sides of which are decorated with the returning spiral pattern, bordered by bands of conventional foliage, thoroughly characteristic of contemporary Italian art, showing the union between Celtic and Roman influence. Its date cannot be later than the end of the seventh century. Bede states that there were no stone fonts in churches in his time. He had

[1] *History of Christian Art,* by Dr. Cutts, p. 97.

evidently never heard of the Deerhurst example, which was in existence in his day. Saxon converts were usually baptized by St. Augustine or St. Paulinus in rivers. Edwin of Northumbria was baptized in a wooden building constructed over a well, and a separate church was erected by Cuthbert, Archbishop of Canterbury, in 750 A.D., near the cathedral, for baptismal purposes. In obedience to the order of the Pope, at the end of the eleventh and during the twelfth century stone fonts were introduced in many churches, sometimes merely rude blocks of stone, hollowed out at the top, and without any sign of sculpture or decoration upon them, while others, like that at Deerhurst, were more elaborate. Some few of these Saxon fonts remain ; most of them have been replaced by those of Norman or later periods, but examples may still be seen at Potterne, Wilts ; Little Billing, Northamptonshire ; Edgmond and Bucknell, Shropshire ; Penmon, Anglesey; and South Hayling, Hampshire.

They are usually placed near the entrance of the church. Some symbolical meaning is attached to this fact, a signification that baptism is the beginning of the Christian life.

It was also a convenience, inasmuch as part of the baptismal service was performed in the porch or outside the door of the church. The manual containing the *ordo ad faciendum catechumenum* directs that this ceremony should be performed *ad valvas ecclesiæ.* The infant was then brought into the church, the priest saying, *Ingredere in templum Dei, ut habeas vitam æternam et vivas in sæcula sæculorum.* After divers other rites the infant was taken to the font and immersed thrice by the priest. The constitutions of Edmund, Archbishop of Canterbury, A.D. 1236, ordered that a font of stone or other durable material, with a fitting cover, should be placed in the churches, and Lyndwood states that it should be large enough for total immersion.

Several fonts were made of lead. In Berkshire we have the interesting leaden Early English font at Childrey, cylindrical in shape, with twelve small mitred figures inscribed upon its surface. Just over the borders of the county, in Oxfordshire, at Dorchester, once the seat of a far-extending bishopric, there is another fine leaden Norman font, with figures of our Lord and the Apostles under semicircular-headed arches. At Warborough, in the same county, there is a similar one, but plainer and of transitional character. Examples of these leaden fonts may also be seen at Brookland, Kent ; Wareham, Dorsetshire; and Walmsford, Northamptonshire.

We have a vast number of Norman fonts in English churches. This may be due to the sanctity and reverence attached to such a holy rite by the builders of later times, who carefully preserved the fountain of regeneration when they rebuilt and altered other parts of the sacred edifice. Paley, in his *Illustrations of Baptismal Fonts*, remarks that the earlier the font the freer the fancy and the more indulgent the genius of the artist. " To the Norman scarcely any object of ordinary observation and contemplation came amiss ; men, animals, fishes, birds, plants, agricultural operations, hunting, hawking ; the saint, the bishop, the priest, the warrior, the heraldic and conventional forms of creatures, living and dead, were worked up with surprising ingenuity and ever-varying forms of delineation. Unquestionably the designers of Norman fonts loved to expatiate in the religious mysticism of the age ; they loved, too, to embody in speaking stone the favourite legends of local saints, and probably also historical incidents. We see here the Serpent overcome, or the salamander, the Baptism of the Saviour and descent of the Holy Dove, the Crucifixion, the Temptation, and other scriptural subjects ; the mystical Vesica Piscis, or the entwined and fretted arms of the floriated cross ; here we find a representation, to us perhaps unintelligible, because the circumstances are unknown, yet evidently descriptive of some mediaeval miracle, or some mighty display of the power of the Church. The fonts of the thirteenth and fourteenth centuries are varied in ingenious devices and in ornamental detail ; but they contain little beyond mere architectural ornaments." Of the later fonts of the Perpendicular period we shall write presently. We will now notice more particularly the artistic skill and workmanship of the Norman masons, trace the legends engraved upon their works, and note the peculiarities of the best examples.

The shapes of Norman fonts vary considerably, and may be classified under eight distinct forms :—

1. Square, without stem, as at West Haddon, Northamptonshire, which is a simple upright square block of stone, about three feet high, with a hemispherical-shaped cavity for a bowl.

2. Square, with a stem, as at Locking, Somerset, a very curious font, remarkable for its sculptured designs.

3. Square, with shafts and central column, as at Palgrave, Suffolk, a late Norman example.

4. Cylindrical, with stem, as at East Haddon.

5. Cylindrical, without stem, as at St. Anne's Church, Lewes, Sussex.

6. Octagonal, without stems and shafts, as at Witham-on-the-Hill, Lincolnshire.

7. Octagonal, with stem or shaft, as at Stibbington, a font of transitional Norman character, but the small pillars supporting the bowl are of later date. There are comparatively few examples of this form. The octagonal shape symbolically represents regeneration, because seven

> days created the old world and the man
> of sin, the eighth day the new man of
> grace and salvation.
>
> 8. Cup-shaped fonts, with or without a stem.
> Thorney, Sussex, furnishes an example
> of the latter, and Plymstock has a good
> specimen of a font with the under side
> rounded off to meet a stem, an interest-
> ing example fashioned of red sandstone
> and adorned with a late Renaissance
> cover.

Many of these Norman fonts are lined with lead, and this practice seems to have been almost universal, except when the stone of which it was fashioned was very hard. It appears that in former times the font was always full of water, and except in the case of granite or marble fonts the water would have percolated through the structure and destroyed the carving. Hence arose the use of covers for fonts, in order to keep the water clean and fresh. Lyndwood suggests that covers were designed in order to ward off magical influences. In Perpendicular times high-towering, spire-like canopies came into fashion, but the early fonts were covered with plain, flat boards, fastened down by staples fixed in the stone. You can still see these staples in some old fonts, or the holes in the stonework in which they were fastened.

Some of these Norman fonts bear inscriptions. Bridekirk, Cumberland, has a font inscribed with

NORMAN FONT, STOKE CANNON, DEVONSHIRE

NORMAN FONT, STANTON FITZWARREN, WILTSHIRE

runic characters. It has some very curious carving, and shows a late survival of the great northern school of sculpture, of which the Saxon crosses at Newcastle and Hexham furnish wonderful examples. This font cannot be earlier than the twelfth century. The church of Stanton Fitz-warren, Wiltshire, has a very curiously inscribed and sculptured font. The bowl is circular, divided by shafts and trefoil arches into ten compartments filled with figures, eight of which represent the triumph of virtues over opposing vices. Opposite the step on which the priest stands is a figure representing the Church, an ecclesiastic crowned, bearing a chalice in his left hand and a cross in his right, and trampling underfoot a dragon. Beside the figure are the words *Serpens occiditur*, and over it is inscribed the word *Ecclesia*. In the next niche is an angel with a drawn sword and enfolding wings, and over it the word *Cherubym*. The other figures represent *Largitas* triumphing over *Avaritia*, *Humilitas* over *Superbia*; *Pietas* over *Discordia* ; *Misericordia* over *Invidia* ; *Modestia* over *Ebrietas* ; *Temperancia* over *Luxuria*; *Paciencia* over *Ira*; and *Pudicitia* over *Libido*. Much skill is shown in the execution of the figures. The upper part is elaborately worked with entwining scroll bands, filled with Norman ornamentation. The font evidently belongs to the Transition period, about the end of the twelfth century. The shaft is much later than the bowl, and evidently belongs to the Decorated period. The height of the font is three feet seven inches, and the diameter two feet eight inches. It is a very rare and curious example.

A very early font at Little Billing, Northamptonshire, bears the name of its sculptor with the inscription : " Wicberhtas artifex atque cementarius hunc fabricavit quiquis suum venit mercere corpus procul dubio capit." The Early English font at Keysoe, Bedfordshire (*circa* 1200 A.D.), has a curious inscription in Norman French, which reads :—

TRESTUI : KEPARDIC I PASSERVI PURLEAL MEWAREL PRIEV : KE
DEVPARSA GRACEVE BREYMERCILIFACE

AM.

This, translated into modern French, signifies :—

Restez : qui par ici passerez,
Pour l'ame de Warel priez :
Que Dieu par sa grace
Voir merci lui fasse.

Amen.

Other instances of inscriptions on fonts need not be here recorded, and I must give some examples of the strange carvings which appear on many of them. At Hook Norton, Oxfordshire, there are representations of Adam and Eve, Sagittarius, and various animals. The famous font at Winchester Cathedral has been a puzzle to antiquaries. It is constructed of a bluish-black calcareous marble, which evidently came from the quarries of Tournai, in Hainault, where the same marble may still be found. Fonts made from this marble also exist at East Meon, St. Michael's, Southampton, St. Mary, Bourne, Lincoln Cathedral, Thornton Curtis, St. Peter's, Ipswich, and there are four others on the Continent. At Zedelghem, near Bruges, is a font very similar to the Winchester example, and the carving shows the same legend, scenes from the life of St. Nicholas of Myra. The story of the saint is well known, how he rescued a king's son from drowning, gave wealth to three daughters of a poor nobleman, saving them from a life of ill-fame, and restored to life three young students who had been slain by a wicked innkeeper, their mutilated bodies having been cast into a tub. On the south and west sides of this Winchester font you see these scenes portrayed in quaint and curious sculpture, while on the north and east sides are symbolic doves and salamanders in three circular medallions. The font is nearly square, and is supported by four detached shafts, adorned with cable mouldings and a heavy central stem. Flowers and leaves, doves drinking from vases from which crosses spring, all conveying symbolical teaching, may also be discovered. The late Dean of Winchester (Dr. Kitchin) concluded that the date of the font cannot be earlier than the twelfth century, from the form of the mitre which appears on the saint's

K

head. The mitre does not appear to have been recognized as part of the episcopal dress until the end of the eleventh century.

The carving on the similar font at East Meon represents the expulsion of Adam and Eve from Paradise and their subsequent instruction in the arts of husbandry and spinning.

At Newenden, Kent, we see some remarkable sculptures : on the north side the representations of a dragon and a lion, and on the west grotesque animals within circles, and on the south a lozenge ornament filled with foliage. At Locking, Somerset, at each angle is a figure in armour with the cylindrical helmet worn about the time of Richard I. The arms of the figures are bent backwards on the side of the bowl, so as to completely surround it, and thus dividing the surface into two compartments, an upper and a lower. These compartments are filled with interlaced work composed of intertwining serpents. The whole font is extremely curious.

There is a strange font at Perranzabuloe, Cornwall. It is octagonal, and four alternate sides are panelled, bearing figures boldly but rudely carved. They are represented in a sitting posture, and clothed in long robes. On the north, west, and south sides are figures representing the Blessed Trinity, that on the east is the Blessed Virgin with the infant Saviour.

A curiously carved font is that at Lenton,

Nottinghamshire. It has suffered many vicissitudes. Tradition states that it formerly belonged to the Priory Church of Lenton, founded in 1100 A.D. by William Peveril, and that it was brought to this church at the dissolution of religious houses. At one time it was presented to a neighbouring gentleman as an ornament for his garden. Happily it has again been restored to the church. The sculptures are curious. On one side is the Crucifixion. A large cross with ends foliated occupies the whole side. Our Lord is on the cross, the soldier piercing His side ; the two malefactors appear on their crosses, and above an angel waving censers. The front is divided into two compartments. In the upper are six angels under canopies, and above them are cherubim. The central arch of the lower compartment contains a representation of the Saviour being taken down from the cross, and on each side are two angels with cherubim similar to those above.

At East Haddon, Northamptonshire, there is a curious figure of a man strangling the necks of serpents. This may signify our Lord bruising the serpent's head, or symbolically represent the conquest over sin by means of baptism.

So great is the number and variety of English fonts of the Norman period that it is only possible in this book to allude to a tithe of those which are most interesting, curious, and important. The example at Avebury, Wilts, is worth noticing. On the east side is carved the figure of a bishop with mitre and crosier, holding a closed book in his left hand ; on each side of him is a dragon whose tail flows off into the foliage which surrounds the upper part, a Norman intersecting arcade running round the lower part. You can still see the marks where the staples of the font cover formerly were.

There is a curious font at Stoke Cannon, Devonshire, totally unlike any other that we have seen elsewhere. The design is bold, the execution rude. The bowl is cylindrical, and is divided into four compartments by weird animals with their heads downwards in a lying posture, their long tails resting beneath their right hind legs. Sculptured crosses and frettes in high relief and of rich design fill the compartments, a cable moulding is on the lower edge. Strange, squat figures of monks with girdles support the bowl with uplifted hands, carved upon the solid stem. The plinth is ornamented with the pelleted star. A quaint and conventional representation of the Nativity appears on the Fincham font, Norfolk ; in one of the panels we see a little crib or manger containing an infant, two diminutive heads of oxen, and a star.

The main characteristics of Early English fonts are the trefoil, sunken arch, the crisp, stiff-leaved foliage, and the other peculiarities of the style, which are observed in the bases and capitals of the shafts and in the deep, hollow mouldings. Strange, grotesque figures are not so common. The sculptors of the thirteenth century took the book of Nature for their study, and the wild, exuberant fancy of the Norman masons no longer finds expression in the works of their successors. During the period of transition we notice the blending of the Norman and Early English details, the dog-tooth moulding, the intersecting Norman arcading, and the Early English trefoil foliage. But traces of the Norman influence soon disappear, and the new style asserts itself. At Rotherfield Greys, Oxfordshire, there is a good example of a perfect Early English font. It is square, the sides diminishing in breadth downwards, the angles being hollowed to receive shafts with foliated capitals which support the round moulding of the upper part. The base is ornamented with the characteristic round and deep hollow mouldings of the style.

Sometimes the design of a font of this period is that of a short Early English clustered pier, the bell capital forming the bowl. Nothing could be simpler or more effective, and the designers of modern fonts for small parish churches could not have a better copy than that of the font at Norbury, Derbyshire. Another excellent model worthy of imitation is the beautiful example at Acton Burnell, Shropshire, octagonal in shape, each side having trefoil-headed recesses and shafts at the angles.

Occasionally an old Norman font has been subsequently carved with Early English foliage and sculpture ; as an example of this process of conversion we may mention the font at Thornbury Church, Gloucestershire. The carving of the circular foliage and cross has puzzled many, who have been led to assign the font to the Transition period ; but it is evident that the sculpture has been wrought by a later hand, and that the font itself is pure Norman work. The example at Lostwithiel, Cornwall, is also rather puzzling. The font is certainly Early English, but the sculpture, representing the Crucifixion, a bishop's head, a grotesque head, two lions passant, a man on horseback with his hawk and hunting-horn, is of Norman style, and was probably copied from some older designs. Sculptured figures are not so common in fonts of the Early English style, but occasionally we meet with them, as at Thorpe, Lincolnshire, where we find finely carved heads of a king, a bishop, and a knight.

As in other spheres of architectural skill, so in the fonts of the Decorated period we find the highest achievements of the mediaeval mason. Beautiful beyond description are some of the examples of fourteenth-century work. You see the richly crocketed canopy, the flowing tracery similar to that which is displayed in the noble and graceful windows of this period of architectural triumphs, the ball-flower ornament, hall-mark of the Decorated style, the diapered ground, the exuberance of niche and sculptured foliage, and the octagonal stem with slender engaged shafts. The bowl itself, in which the water of regeneration lies, was the main object upon which the fourteenth-century artist lavished all his care and skill. That he enriched with all the highest achievements of his art. The stem was left plain and unadorned. When faith waxed feebler, and art was loved more for its own sake than as a handmaid to religion, stem and bowl received a like treatment.

A fine and perfect example of early Decorated work is the font at Goadly, Marwood, Leicestershire. It is octagonal, and on each face is the form and tracery of a Decorated window. There is a slight variation in this tracery, no two sides being exactly alike. The simple round moulding characteristic of the period is employed with admirable effect. Another beautiful example is the font at Patrington, East Yorkshire, with its crocketed canopies and delicate carving. At Wortham, too, in Suffolk, there is a very beautiful Decorated font. It is octagonal, and each side contains a triangular, crocketed canopy, the heads of which and the spandrels are enriched with foliated circles. The angles have buttresses supported by heads, and the top is doubly battlemented. Somewhat similar, but more delicate, is the font at Hedon, Yorkshire, with its cinquefoiled arches under rich crocketed ogee canopies and spandrels filled with foliage and ornaments.

Not infrequently we find in Decorated fonts the absence of a supporting shaft, the octagonal form being continued down to the plinth, as at Exton, Rutlandshire. Figures are rare in the examples of this period, but occasionally we meet with the evangelistic emblems and other designs. On the font at Stoke Golding, Leicestershire, appear the figures of St. Katherine with the wheel and sword, St. Margaret with a book in her right hand and a pastoral staff in her left, trampling on a dragon, and on her left side a kneeling figure of a child and a bishop under a canopy. On two sides of the font are shields. Towards the end of the Decorated period and during the prevalence of the Perpendicular style, heraldic shields become much more common. You do not find them in earlier work. The introduction of these shields reveals perhaps a decay of faith, the desire to perpetuate the honour of a name or family rather than to promote the honour of the Deity. "The boast of heraldry, the pomp of power" began to obtrude themselves in the offerings of the rich men of the time. No longer were beauty and art to be sought for and consecrated to the worship of God, but the name and power of the family were to be stamped upon the offering. This is, perhaps, the story that these armorial bearings tell.

At Norwich, in the Church of All Saints, there is a fine octagonal example with each side adorned with two well-executed figures in high relief. They represent the twelve Apostles, St. Paul, St. John the Baptist, St. Michael, and St. George. The shaft, too, is richly ornamented with figures in canopied recesses, with foliage and interlacing stalks. One of them represents St. Lawrence, the others I am unable to identify.

When the Decorated period is passing away during the age of transition the panelling of the Perpendicular style is gradually developed. The fonts at Cricklade, Wilts, at Penton, Hampshire, at Poynings, Sussex, furnish examples of this. The style which prevailed during the Perpendicular period shows a certain sameness and repetition of device, but the execution is wonderfully fine and the sculpture beautiful. The ornamentation differs from that of the preceding periods. Heraldic achievements are more frequently met with. Séjant lions, evangelistic emblems, shields, the seven sacraments, the instruments of the Passion, are some of the favourite subjects selected by the fifteenth-century masons. More attention is paid to the stem, which is now panelled, while angels with outspread wings sometimes appear in the part nearest the bowl.

Perpendicular builders loved to raise their fonts on high, the approach being by several steps, and to cover them with large, high, towering, spire-like covers. Examples of them occur at Ewelme, Oxfordshire ; Elsing, Suffolk ; Castleacre, Norfolk ; and Frieston, Lincolnshire.

We will examine the details of some of these Perpendicular fonts. There is a large and noble font at North Somercotes, Lincolnshire. It is octagonal, and on five sides there are shields bearing arms, and on the other three are the emblems of the Passion and a figure representing the Resurrection. The emblems of the Passion are the four nails, hammers, scourges, crown of thorns, spear, reed, and sponge. They appear again on the beautiful font at Covenham St. Mary, in the same county.

The Tudor flower often appears on fonts of this period. Inscriptions become more frequent than in the earlier fonts. At Bourne, Lincolnshire, the font bears the legend in black letter inscribed on the sides, each word in a separate compartment :—

Ihs Est nomē qōe sūp ome nōm.[1]

Round the upper part of the octagonal basin of the rich font at St. Mary, Beverley, Yorkshire, we find inscribed :—

Pray for the soules of Wyllm Feryffaxe Draper
and his wyvis which made this font of his pper costes
the x day of Marche ye year of our Lord MCIIII.

[1] This inscription written in full reads : *Jesus est nomen quod est super omne nomen.*

At Walsoken, Norfolk, a richly carved example bears two inscriptions. Beneath the figures carved on the stem are the words :—

Remeber ye soul of S. Ihonyter and
Margaret his wife and
John Beforth Chapli

and below this on the base appears the following :—

Anno Dni mill quig inte qua Drge qrto

The whole design is most elaborate, buttresses, pinnacles, ogee arches, minute panels, etc., crowding upon each other and producing the effect of excessive ornamentation. On the sides of the bowl are representations of the Crucifixion and the seven sacraments, supported by brackets formed of foliage and angels. Figures of saints adorn the stem, St. John, St. Margaret, St. Paul, and others, and on the base are the emblems of the Passion.

East Anglia can boast of many famous Perpendicular fonts, and amongst these there is a remarkable series of examples which vary so little that they must have been the work of one craftsman. The Church of St. John, Sepulchre, at Norwich ; Saxlingham, Hales, Blickling, All Saints, and St. Mary, Shotesham, and Leveringham all contain fonts of similar style and character. The panels on the bowl contain the evangelistic emblems and angels bearing shields, supported by angels with expanded wings. The stem is octagonal, having small buttresses at four of the angles and between these lions séjant.

Many other examples might be given of the elaborate fonts of the fifteenth century and of the curious covers erected in Elizabethan or Jacobean times. The wondrous cover of the font at Lanreath, Cornwall, with its rich characteristic Jacobean carving, is a good specimen of the style of the period, and there is a very elaborate cover to the Norman font at Plymstock of about the same time, octagonal in shape, with the figure of a saint on each alternate side painted in colours. The cover at Ewelme is very magnificent, its spiral form with its numerous arches, buttresses, and pinnacles rising towards the roof. It possesses the over-elaborateness of the later Perpendicular style, and consists of four tiers of arches ending in a richly crocketed spire, and surmounted by a figure of St. Michael. These heavy covers, which must create fears in the heart of the priest when he is officiating, are usually drawn up by pulleys ; but sometimes they are fixed, and a small door in the side admits to the interior of the font.

St. Alban's Abbey once possessed a brass font, in which, according to Camden's *Britannia* (1586) the children of the kings of Scotland used to be baptized. It was presented to the church by Sir Richard Lee, who received a grant of the abbey and its lands at the dissolution of the monasteries. This font was taken away at the time of the great civil war by " one Hickman, a vile ironmonger, a justice of the peace proper for those times." Fuller records that it " was taken away in the late cruel war, as it seems, by those hands which suffered nothing how sacred soever to stand, which could be converted to money. There is a wooden one to supply its place, which is said to be made of the same shape with the old font." A marble font was at one time substituted for this wooden one, and may still be seen in the abbot's cloister, and a modern one has now taken its place.

Considering the periods of storm and plunder through which our churches have passed, the icono-clastic zeal of the Puritans, the desecration during the civil war when soldiers and steeds encamped in the sacred precincts, the destruction wrought at the Reformation, the times of laxity and care-lessness and of ignorant and perverse " restora-tion," it is wonderful that so many of our ancient fonts have been preserved and remain to us as a glorious heritage, relics of the earnest faith and artistic skill of our forefathers, and as models for future work.

CHAPTER X

WINDOWS AND STAINED GLASS

NO part of our church is more important and interesting than the windows and the glass that fills them, displaying—

An art that is
The incarnation of the sublime.

In our typical church there are examples of all ages. A little Saxon window shows itself near the porch. It has a double splay, that is to say, the window is not flush with the exterior wall, but is set midway between the outside and inside surface. It is round-headed, and the width of the surrounding arch is greater at the bottom than it is at the point just below the curved head. Saxon and Norman windows are usually small, and the churches must have been very dark. Indeed, there seems always to have been a craving for light—more light, as the ages progressed, perhaps a symbolical representation of the eager searching after increased spiritual light and education characteristic of the soul of man.

Norman windows are small and narrow, round-headed, but the actual window is now almost flush with the outside wall and the recess in which it is placed is splayed only on the interior side.   In large churches the windows of this period are of greater size, but usually in our village churches they are such as I have described.   The Norman masons often decorated them on the interior as they did their doors with small shafts, while the arches are ornamented with zigzag and other Norman mouldings.   The altar was often lighted by three of these windows placed close together, and in the clerestory are round windows of this period.   During the latter part of the twelfth century and the beginning of the thirteenth the round arch disappeared and the lancet form of window was constructed.   These Early English windows are long and narrow, resembling in form the surgeon's lancet, whence they take their name. But the worshippers wanted more light.   Hence the masons placed two of these windows together under a single-arched dripstone, and pierced the space at the head with a round or lozenge-shaped opening.   Thus we have a window corresponding in some measure with those of a later date, which with their elaborate tracery are only developments of the simple idea of plate tracery devised by the Early English masons.

Improving upon this, the fourteenth-century artificers increased the number of lights, divided them by narrower strips of stone-work called mullions, and filled the head with graceful and elaborate tracery of much beauty and diversity. In my handbook on Gothic architecture I have tried to describe some of the varying forms of decorated tracery, geometrical, reticulated, flamboyant, Kentish, and the rest, and need not repeat such descriptions here.

Again the cry for more light was raised, and the fifteenth-century folk were very proud of their skill, and hesitated not to pull out windows of an earlier age erected by their forefathers, and to insert larger windows in the style known as Perpendicular. They loved panel decoration, and everything was made to conform to the idea of panels. Thus they carried up the mullions straight through the head of the window to the arch, divided the head into panel-shaped compartments, and introduced transoms, or horizontal pieces of stonework dividing the lights and giving additional opportunities for their favourite panels. They introduced larger square-headed windows into the clerestory, and the light of the sun shone into the church more brightly and clearly than it had ever done before.

There is a mysterious-looking window on the south side of the chancel quite low down, which does not seem to correspond with any other. This is called a " low side window," and has been a puzzle to antiquaries for many years as to its object and use. It is usually denominated a leper's window, and lively imaginations have pictured these poor distressed folk, who were forbidden from entering a church, coming to this window in order to gain comfort from the sight of the celebration of the holy mysteries, or kneeling on the turf to confess their sins to the priest and obtain the benefit of absolution. This idea must be erroneous, as the poor lepers were not allowed even to enter a churchyard. Some think that they were used for persons outside to see the elevation of the Host, just as the squints were used in the interior of the church ; but these windows are so placed that it is impossible for any one outside to see the celebrant. Another idea is that they were used as confessionals, the priest in the church hearing the confession of the penitent who knelt on the grass in the churchyard. A more inconvenient arrangement could not have been devised, and this idea might at once be dismissed, were it not that one of the commissioners of Henry VIII appointed to suppress monasteries and chantries wrote : " We think it best that the place where these friars have been wont to hear outside confessions of all-comers at certain times of the year be walled up, and that use to be done for ever." It appears, therefore, that sometimes, at any rate, these low-side windows were used for this purpose. However, I am inclined to think that they were intended for the use of anchorites or recluses, who sometimes took up their abode in churches.

L

They were not glazed, as they now are, but had iron bars on the outside and a wooden shutter on the inside of the church, and were probably the means of communication of these anchorites with the outside world.

It is impossible, however, to dogmatize upon a subject which has puzzled antiquaries for many years. In the *Antiquary* (May, 1890), there were expressions of opinion by many distinguished authorities published in a form that was called " a Conference " upon the object of these windows, and some whose judgment is of weight, including the learned editor, Dr. Cox, expressed the belief that they were used for the sounding of the sanctus bell by a server when the Host was elevated. In opposition to the theory with regard to anchorites it may be urged that there are countless churches which have low-side windows, and it may be doubted whether each one had an anchorite dwelling in it. There are some which have reclusoria or cells, as at Compton in Surrey, and we should like to describe them ; but want of space prevents us from dwelling on objects which are so rare and exceptional. I may mention, however, that these anchor-holds, or reclusoria, were chambers or cells wherein dwelt pious folk who wished to retire from the world and live alone a life of devotion. Examples may be seen at Chester-le-Court, Warkworth, Morpeth, and Thirsk, and an illustration of such a chamber at Rettenden

is given in Cutts's *Scenes from the Middle Ages.*
Sometimes there were anchor-holds in churchyards.
We sigh to think of the solitary life of these
recluses, but they were a little lax sometimes, and
Bishop Poore compares a peering anchoress to
" an untamed bird in a cage," and sometimes they
used to gossip at the window and even to speak
to men and to have friends, and lived on the gifts
of the charitable.   Perhaps the life of a recluse
was not so severe and miserable as we imagine.

The stained glass in the windows is often deplor-
able.   The art of producing it not very long ago
had sunk to an apparently hopeless state of de-
cadence, and nothing could be more hideous than
the terrible productions of the eighteenth and early
nineteenth centuries.   Many of our churches are
still disfigured by examples of the art of that
debased period, but our own day has witnessed an
extraordinary revival.   The old secrets have been
discovered anew, and there is no longer any lost
art.   But happily all the work of the ancient
artists has not vanished, and a study of it illus-
trates very clearly the faith, history, and cunning
craft of our forefathers who attained to such high
achievements.

The first use of coloured glass for windows
dates from very early times.   Glass in frames
was found at Pompeii.   The windows of St. Sophia
are said to have been filled with coloured glass
set in cut alabaster openings, a practice still in

vogue in the East. Coloured glass placed in lead is probably a French, or rather Norman, invention, as is also that of painted glass. In Saxon times the art found a home in England, the *artifices lapidearum et vitrearum fenestrarum* having been invited to this country by Wilfrid, Archbishop of York, in 709 A.D. The earliest specimen of ancient stained glass now in existence is to be found at Le Mans and is of the eleventh century ; the earliest English example is believed to be in the choir aisles of Canterbury Cathedral, where it was probably fixed when the church was rebuilt after the fire in 1174. But the whole art of stained glass was essentially Gothic. It began with the rise of Gothic architecture, or perhaps with the Byzantine and Romanesque out of which it was just emerging ; it continued to follow all the glories of the thirteenth, fourteenth, and fifteenth centuries, and began to decline in the sixteenth century. The revival of the art is due to the revival of the love of Gothic which the closing years of the nineteenth century witnessed.

Chiddingfold seems to have been the only place in England where glass was made prior to 1563, and then only plain green glass, not the coloured glass, was manufactured. All the latter seems to have been imported, and Normandy and Lorraine and Bohemia were the early seats of the industry. The green tint of the Chiddingfold and other early glass was caused by the presence of iron in the sand.   Twelfth and thirteenth-century glass has a horny appearance, and bubbles and streaks appear in it, which, though defects in manufacture, do not diminish its beauty.   The principal colours used in this early glass were ruby, blue, various shades of green, a deep yellow, and a purple-brown.   In the fourteenth century yellow produced by silver stain, a more delicate stain than that used earlier, was discovered, and in the following century the method of coating one colour over another was adopted, thus producing new colours and a variety of shades.   Rose pink produced from gold was discovered in the sixteenth century.   It is possible to tell the age of a window by glancing at the preponderating colours shown therein.   Thus in the twelfth and thirteenth century red and blue appear, in the fourteenth century yellow and green, and in the Perpendicular period red and blue with white, of a purer texture than before, and purple.   The Renaissance introduced painting upon clear glass, and the use of vitreous enamel revolutionized the art.

Let us now consider more closely the characteristics of the various styles, which have produced such wondrous windows—

<blockquote>
Chaste, subdued
In lights and shadows ; dimming the world beyond
And shading the Eternal House of God.
</blockquote>

Happily much has been spared to us, though the destruction has been great.   During the

Reformation many windows were broken, on the ground that they treated of " superstitious " subjects. Some glass was buried and disinterred in less troubled times. Cromwell's soldiers destroyed much when they ransacked our churches and left them—

> Shorn of their glass of a thousand colourings,
> Through which the deepened glories once could enter.

In later times priceless old glass has been removed in order to give place to the feeble and degenerate productions of early Victorian artists. But fortunately much has been left both in England and on the Continent, where the lover of stained glass will make many a devout pilgrimage.

The story of stained glass corresponds with that of the architecture of our churches, and as the style of architecture changed, so the art of the glass-painter changed with it. But the change was not quite simultaneous, and the latter lingered on a little longer after the former had begun to alter its characteristic features. We may divide the periods of stained glass into Early Gothic, which lasted to the close of the thirteenth century ; Decorated Gothic, which embraced the fourteenth century ; and Perpendicular Gothic (corresponding to the Flamboyant in France and the Florid in Germany), the fifteenth and part of the sixteenth century, until it was replaced by the Renaissance. We will examine the style and features of each period.

I. Early Gothic

In this period the colours used were very rich, and the designs consisted of medallions containing subjects taken from Holy Scripture, or the lives of the saints, upon grounds of ruby and blue. Mosaic patterns form the groundwork of the medallions, and a border of scrolls and foliage encloses the whole design. The glazier's art was then at its zenith, and the painting was subsidiary to the leading. Pieces of pot-metal glass were laboriously cut into shades. The foliage and decoration were conventional, and followed the design of the late Norman or Early English patterns, familiar to students of architecture. Figure windows are not uncommon in Early Gothic work. The architectural framework which develops itself in succeeding styles is now insignificant, the drawing of the figures rude and archaic, and the artist seems to have aimed chiefly at obtaining a blaze of brilliant colour. Bits of white glass are introduced to represent eyes, and the flesh is a reddish brown. Medallion windows are typical of the Early Gothic style. Jesse windows were favourites during all the mediaeval period ; in this style the " vine " is not a vine, but its leaves and fruit are in accordance with the conventional types of thirteenth-century foliage. It would require, however, a separate chapter for the full consideration of the origin and development of the Jesse window. We may sum up the virtues of these Early Gothic artists, whose names have passed away, but much of whose work remains. They tried for and obtained the glorious effects of splendid colouring by the aid of their wonderful mosaics of small fragments of glass, and cared not to use paint, except in so far as it was necessary to represent a figure, tell the story of his life, or to supply detail to their ornamental work. Their glazing was wonderful and never surpassed ; their painting was rude and conventional, but they were true artists, triumphed over many details of construction and manipulation, and laid the foundations of the art which subsequent years developed. You will find some examples of twelfth-century work at York and Canterbury, and in several churches in France. Of thirteenth-century work many of the great French churches retain examples, notably Chartres, Bourges, Le Mans, and the Sainte Chapelle, Paris. In England we have the Five Sisters at York, medallion windows at Canterbury, and other examples at Lincoln and Salisbury and in several village churches, which in spite of many changes still retain good examples of the skill of the Early English artist. We give illustrations of some glass of this period at Aldermaston.

II. Decorated Gothic

To the altered conditions of architecture, the increased size of windows, and the variety of design

THE CORONATION OF THE VIRGIN

THE ANNUNCIATION

WINDOWS AT ALDERMASTON CHURCH, BERKSHIRE

which Decorated Gothic introduced, the glass artist
had to adapt himself. He admired, too, the new,
natural foliage which the sculptor had introduced
instead of the conventional leaves of his forefathers,
and was careful to imitate this in his painting.
The larger windows suggested to him that he might
make use of this increased space. No longer
hampered by small, narrow windows, his ideas
expanded, and he was ambitious enough to paint
large pictures spreading over several lights. He
stained the white glass yellow, and changed the
dark, sombre hues of his predecessor into brighter
colours. Windows were often divided into
diamond-shaped quarries, and a pattern of trailing
natural foliage painted on them. Heavy canopies
after the style of the Decorated period tower above
the figures. Horizontal bars, of course, stretched
across the glass, and these with the mullions naturally formed compartments. This space invited the
artist to draw separate designs. If the space was
too small he extended his picture across the mullion
into the adjoining compartment, which leads to
confusion in trying to interpret the design. Thus
in one compartment you will see a figure of the
Virgin kneeling, and in the adjoining light an
angel bearing a scroll inscribed " Ave Maria." In
the next period we shall see that the painters began
entirely to neglect the mullion ; for example, they
would paint the extended arms of our Saviour
crucified in the lights adjoining that which contains

His sacred body. But that unfortunate convention was not yet. The canopy placed over the heads of the figures usually occurs, the shafts of which were carried down on each side, but occasionally architectural landscapes were devised, which were greatly developed in the next period. In fact, this period of the art was an age of transition. We are accustomed to regard the fourteenth century as the period of the perfection of the triumphs of architecture, but it was not that of the glass artist. He was feeling his way. He had left behind the barbaric splendour and wealth of colour of the preceding period, and had not attained to the perfection of his art. That was left to his successor. In the meantime he wrought carefully and well, and did wonders, adapting himself to the changed conditions of the architecture. The tracery of the upper parts of the windows presented difficulties in the filling in of the smaller and variously shaped openings. We see the little figures of angels or heads of saints which he devised, and usually they are well adapted in size and drawing to the space which they were required to fill. Heraldic shields he also found useful, when the influence of " the boast of heraldry, the pomp of power," began to make itself felt in architectural ornamentation. As the century progressed the figure drawing improved, and the process of stippling was discovered, which added much to the beauty of the windows.

The best Decorated glass in England is found in the nave and Chapterhouse at York, in Wells, Merton College, Oxford, Bristol, Tewkesbury, and Gloucester.

III. LATE GOTHIC

With the advent of the Perpendicular style in England the glass-painter had again to adapt himself to changed conditions, and here he parted company with his French brother, who was busy filling the fantastic, flamelike apertures of the Flamboyant Gothic windows. He was required to fill the panelled spaces which the fifteenth-century English architect devised, and the most satisfactory method seemed to be the introduction of canopied figures. His aim was to produce a better picture and to introduce more light. He ceased to be a glazier, or to rely on glazing, and strove to be a painter. He thought of his painting first, the glazing was an afterthought. He loved white glass, and in the canopies of his figures he introduced a large amount of this, as he knew that it was the best sort of glass on which to work in order to give the best effect to his art. He also knew that these white canopies would show off and act as a good frame to his rich figure work. He placed white glass also at the foot of the figure for the same purpose, and this he painted so as to form a niche, in which he placed some scene from the saint's life to illustrate his subject. A white nimbus sometimes surrounds the saint's head. The smaller panel-like openings in the head of the window are treated in the same way as the larger lights, save that the figures are of course smaller. In France floating angels with outspread wings fill the Flamboyant openings.

The fifteenth-century artist now began to use the whole window with all its lights for a single subject. You can see in the background landscapes, trees, churches, towers, and castles and blue sky, or a vaulted room and a glimpse of sky and scenery through an opening arch. The English artist differed from his continental brother in using light-coloured glass. Abroad rich and deep colouring was still fashionable.

England possesses some of the best glass of this period, though we owe some debt to foreign workers. The great Florentine artist, Francesco di Lievi da Gambassi, visited this country, and there is a letter dated 1434, written " to the master glass-painter Gambessi, then in Scotland, and who made works in glass of various kinds, and was held to be the best glass painter in the world." How much must we regret the destruction by fanatical mobs of the windows made by this excellent artist for Holyrood Chapel and other churches ! But we have much fine glass of this period, notably at New College, Merton, and All Souls, Oxford, and at Winchester, at York Minster, and other churches in that city, Great Malvern, and Fairford ; the latter are probably English, though legend tells of a German source.   Good Flemish glass appears at St. Mary's, Shrewsbury, and in the little church of Shiplake, Oxfordshire, which once adorned the ruined church of St. Bertin at St. Omer, plundered during the French Revolution.

We should like to dwell upon some of the good Renaissance windows, many of which retain the Gothic spirit, but the attractions of the mediaeval style have kept us too long, and prevent us from touching upon the perfections of the later artists and the gradual decline and decay of the art.

It has now happily revived and the productions of the best glass painters of the twentieth century vie with those of the brightest period of mediaeval art.   It is well, however, to look back upon the progress of the art, to see again the craftsmen and artists of the Middle Ages manipulating their paints, their glass and tools, and from the study of their methods to form new ideas and conceptions of artistic merit and possibilities, and to learn new arts by investigating the old.

CHAPTER XI

ROOD-SCREENS AND LOFTS

IT is quite possible that your village church possesses a beautiful rood-screen separating the nave from the chancel. If you live in Devonshire or East Anglia the chances are favourable to its existence, but there are many churches in different parts of England and on the Welsh border where they remain. There is a very charming one at Warfield, in Berkshire, at Hurst, in the same county, and a curious one much adorned with painting at North Crawley, in Buckinghamshire. They are usually of wood and are beautifully carved. If the screen has been destroyed, you will frequently find evidence of its former presence. Close to one of the pillars supporting the chancel arch there are the remains of a staircase that formerly led to the rood-loft. Corbels are visible on each side of the arch, which at one time supported the rood-beam, on which there stood a large crucifix with the figures of St. Mary the Virgin and St. John on either side. Above the place of the rood there is sometimes a decorated ceiling to mark the sanctity of the rood and the reverence attached to it. The lower part of the screen is usually composed of traceried panels separated into groups of four by triplet shafts, with a band of curved ornament on either side, the shafts extending upwards to take the ribs of the small fan-shaped wooden vault above, while the ornament carries the lower rib of the vault, intersecting at its apex the ornament from the adjoining post. At the bottom of each panel is a quatrefoil with a carved leaf in the centre of it ; the upper part is filled with tracery. On these panels figures were painted, and many of them we can recognize by their symbols. There is a figure of St. Peter with the inscription : *Credo in Deum Patrem, omnipotentem, creatorem,* that being the article in the Creed which tradition ascribes to him. We recognize the figure of St. James the Great by the inscription : *Qui conceptus est de Spiritu Sancto, natus ex Maria Virgine.* St. George is known by his treading on the dragon ; St. Cecilia by her harp and book. There are figures of other saints, but some have perished, and others have been spoilt by restoration.

Above the panels are the main pierced tracery bay divisions of the screen. From about two-thirds of its height a small moulded capital takes the springing of the small vault ribs. Between the ribs the vault is enriched with sunk tracery, or sometimes with fruit or foliage carved in low relief. In the sixteenth-century screens, heads and other

Renaissance details often appear. A marvellous cornice crowns the whole, having several orders of what Mr. F. Bligh Bond calls "vignette enrichment," divided by strips of beading, and the whole finished at the top with delicate cresting. Originally all this beautiful work was painted with dull red, greens and gold, but now only little spots of colour can be seen to reveal in a vague way its once glorious appearance. The sides of the chancel are separated from the aisle chapels by smaller screens or parcloses.

We must imagine above the screen the great crucifix with its attendant figures, which sometimes rested upon the space above the fan vault called the rood-loft, and in other cases were fastened to a separate heavy beam that spanned the chancel arch, called the rood-beam. Before the rood a light was kept always burning, and the rood-loft was the place for village musicians and an organ, if the church boasted of one. An altar also stood below the cross. If there was no chancel arch the space between the loft and the roof was usually boarded up, forming a tympanum and a background to the rood. This was generally painted with some such subject as the Doom, which in later times has been plastered over and subsequently rediscovered.

If your church can boast of such a beautiful structure, it will closely resemble that which I have tried to describe. Of course there are some diversities in details, but most of these screens are based upon the above model.

If you would know the object and *raison d'être* of these rood-screens you cannot do better than study an excellent article written by Mr. Aymer Vallance for a book edited by me, the *Memorials of Old Kent*. He shows that from the earliest times there was a custom of screening off the chancel from the nave. As our order of Divine service can in some details be traced back to the old Jewish synagogue worship, it may be that the idea of screening off the chancel, where the holy mysteries are celebrated, arose from the plan of the old temple, wherein the Holy of Holies was hidden from the eyes of worshippers by an impenetrable veil. In olden days the altar was hidden by a veil during Lent, and we have seen in a Berkshire church the pulley which caused this veil to be raised or lowered. This shutting off of the chancel, this " Holy of Holies," was, therefore, no new idea. In many of our cathedrals we have large stone screens of very substantial structure, adorned with niches for statues and canopy work ; and stone screens are occasionally met with in country churches, as in our little Berkshire church of Baulking, and there is a fine one at Stebbing and Great Bardfield, in Essex. Of wooden screens the oldest in the country is said, in Mr. F. Harrison's *Notes on Sussex Churches*, to be the somewhat plain example at old Shoreham,

M

in Sussex, the tracery of which dates back to the end of the thirteenth century. But this is not correct, as the curious church at Compton, in Surrey, is at least a century older, and is of Norman character. Visitors to that remarkable building will remember the curious arrangement in the chancel, which has an upper chapel above a lower one. The screen stands at the west side of the former, and consists of a series of round-headed arches supported by small octagonal shafts. The screen at Stanton Harcourt is also very ancient, and is of thirteenth-century date. When examining it we found some holes pierced through the lower panels, and we were asked the purpose of these holes. We ventured to suggest that they might have been used for hearing confessions ; but Dr. Cox assures us that this surmise is incorrect, and holds that they were miniature squints for worshippers to see the altar and the elevation of the Host. Most of these wooden screens date back to the fifteenth century. There are several particu-larly interesting screens in the churches on the Welsh border, notably at Llananno, Radnorshire ; Llandefalle, Breconshire ; Partrishow, Llanvilo, and Llangurig ; but several of the lofts escaped destruction, as the churches are situate in remote and mountainous districts, and the screens did not fall a prey to such wretches as Dowsing, who committed so many enormities in East Anglia. Partrishow has retained not only its screen and

HANDBOROUGH, OXFORDSHIRE

CHARLTON-ON-OXMOOR, OXFORDSHIRE

CHANCEL SCREENS

loft with traceried panels finely carved, but in the angles formed by the screen and the walls of the nave there remain two rood-screen altars, each with its *mensa,* upon which the five crosses of consecration may be traced.

The roods which set forth the Passion of our Lord fell a prey to reforming zeal in the reign of Edward VI, when an order was issued for their destruction. This was obeyed with thoroughness, and only one mutilated set of the figures of the Saviour, St. Mary the Virgin, and St. John exists in the Powysland museum, whither they were conveyed from the church of Mochdre, in Montgomeryshire. The cross has vanished, but the head and body of Christ remain, shorn of arms and feet. The head is crowned with thorns, the hair falling down upon the shoulders, the brow is deeply furrowed, and the face shows an expression of pain. The Virgin wears a long flowing robe with a veil and a cloak, and she was apparently crowned. The wood is much decayed, but there are traces of colour, white, gold, and vermilion.

This seems to be the only surviving relic of the countless roods that once adorned our churches. When these were destroyed many of the figures of saints were obliterated and replaced by texts of Scripture, the Ten Commandments, or the royal arms. In Elizabeth's time rood-lofts were condemned, but the order was only partially obeyed. The Devonshire folk liked not the changes wrought by the introduction of the Book of Common Prayer, and rose in rebellion against the authorities. They loved their screens, which their own hands had fashioned. Hence it was not deemed prudent to disturb them. In East Anglia, where Puritanism developed in later days and Dowsing made his iconoclastic pilgrimages, many suffered, though happily some survived, which still delight our eyes when we wander through the counties of Norfolk, Suffolk, Essex, and Cambridgeshire.

There still remain about a thousand of these screens in English churches, and it would be quite impossible within the limits of this book to attempt to describe them, but the reader will find a complete list of them given in that interesting volume of the *Antiquary's Books* which deals with Church Furniture, and sundry articles by Mr. Aymer Vallance in the series of memorials on the counties of England.

We may notice that the introduction of screens in the fifteenth century often necessitated some structural alterations in the church. A window was often placed high up on the north side to give light to the rood, and perhaps one of the reasons why the fifteenth-century builders were so fond of introducing a large window on the south was to display the beauties of the screen. Moreover, it was necessary to gain access to the loft, to light the rood lamp and candles, and for the musicians to climb to their accustomed place. Hence the staircase had to be constructed, which is often contained in an added turret to the arch on the north or south side. In Wales they were often content with a ladder.

It is, however, time to pass on to examine other features of our church, and to leave the contemplation of rood-screens and lofts.

CHAPTER XII

LECTERNS

ON the south of the screen stands the lectern, now used for holding the Bible for the reading of the Lessons. Possibly a modern brass eagle-shaped desk has been substituted for the ancient lectern, and your church will be fortunate if it retains its former one. In pre-Reformation days it stood in the middle of the choir, and held the service book or chanter, from which the chanters, arranged on either side of it, chanted the services, as we have seen in the great church of the Duomo at Florence. In early times in Italy there were fixed desks for the reading of the Gospel and the Epistle, and that which bore the book of the Gospels was shaped as an eagle with outstretched wings, the symbol of St. John the Evangelist. It is equally appropriate for the bearing of the Bible, the Word of God, carried as on eagles' wings to the four corners of the earth, and raising our thoughts that fly, like the flight of the eagle, heavenwards. The earliest mention of a lectern proves that this was the usual pattern. It is recorded that St. Eloy made a copper eagle for the Abbey of St. Hilaire at Poictiers about the beginning of the seventh century, and that when King Dagobert sacked the city of Poictiers he carried it off with him. Indeed, from this accustomed form lecterns obtained the name of " eagles." In England these desks were in early times made of wood, of which an interesting example remains at Blythburgh, Suffolk, of the date 1452. It has a double desk, revolving on a central stem, which is adorned with miniature buttresses, the foot resembling the base of a Perpendicular pier. In the gable-shaped space between the twin desks there is a quatrefoil opening with a carved leaf ornament in the centre, and the summit is crowned with a sort of Tudor flower cresting. There is an Early Decorated lectern at East Hendred, in Berkshire, of curious design, the stem being shaped like a foot resting on the head of a dragon, emblematical of the Word of God conquering the powers of evil. Most of the early eagle lecterns were introduced in the Perpendicular period, but many of them fell a prey to the pillagers of churches at the Reformation, and it was not until the Restoration of king and Church in the seventeenth century that this model was revived.

Some of the early lecterns have had extraordinary adventures. There is a fine brass eagle at the Church of St. Stephen, St. Albans, which was presented to the chapel of Holyrood at Edinburgh about 1530. Soon after this, in 1544, the

Earl of Hertford made a raid over the Scottish border and burned the palace and chapel. Amongst his commanders was Sir Richard Lee, who carried this lectern with a brass font back to England, and presented the former to St. Stephen's Church and the latter to St. Alban's Abbey. The Reformation soon dawned, and the pillaging of churches ensued. The font was sold, but the vicar buried the old lectern beneath the chancel floor, where it was recently accidentally discovered. It bears some arms and the inscription *Georgius Creichtown Episcopus Dunkeldensis* (1527-1550).

Another adventurous lectern is that at South-well, which formerly belonged to the monks of Newstead Abbey. When misfortune fell upon this monastery at the time of the Dissolution, the monks placed their most precious charters in the stem of the lectern and threw it into a fishpond, hoping in better days to recover it. They never lived to do so, but it was discovered later on and has found an abiding home in the Minster. There is a very interesting post-Reformation wooden lectern at the church of St. Nicholas, Islip, in Oxfordshire. It is quite plain, and consists of a double desk on a stem, with places for books beneath it. It was placed there when the witty Dr. Robert South restored the church in 1680.

In some churches there is a little stone reading desk near the font for the holding of the office book, and also stone Gospel lecterns let into the north wall of the chancel. Another lectern was needed in the church for the accommodation of the Bible and some other books which, after the Reformation, were ordered to be placed in churches for the people to read and study. These books were often chained, lest they should be carried away by too eager students. Racks to hold the books and dcsks on which to place them are to be found in many churches. At Chelsea we find the Bible, Prayer Book, and the Homilies still chained to the desk, above which is a receptacle for the books. Amongst the books so provided for the instruction of the congregation in the days when cheap books were unknown and public libraries were not, are the works of Erasmus, Jewel, Foxe's *Book of Martyrs*, the Homilies, Calvin, and several others, recalling an era long since past.

CHAPTER XIII

MURAL PAINTINGS

NO part of the ancient decoration of our churches has suffered more than the paintings and frescoes which formerly adorned their walls. In the whole of the country there are comparatively few of the ancient edifices which retain any traces of the numerous quaint designs and figures painted on the inner surfaces of their walls during the mediaeval period. Our ancestors used to make free use of colour for the purposes of architectural decoration, and employed several means in order to produce the effect. They sometimes used fresco, by means of which they produced pictures upon walls covered with plaster while the plaster was wet. Sometimes they employed wall painting, i.e. they covered the walls when the plaster was dry with some pictorial representation. The distinction between fresco and wall painting is frequently forgotten. Most of the early specimens of this art are monochromes, but subsequently the painters used polychrome, which signifies surface colouring by means of various hues. The vaulted ceilings, the timber roof, the screens and canopies, the monuments with their effigies, as well as the surface of the walls, were often coloured with diaper-work. Colour and gilding were marked features in all mediaeval buildings, and even richly carved fonts and sculptured monuments were embellished by this method of decoration. The appearance of our churches in those times must have been very different from what it is now. Then a blaze of colour met the eye on entering the sacred building ; the events and characters of sacred history were brought to mind by the representations upon the walls, and the days of hideous whitewash and bare walls had not yet dawned. Only a few years ago in a certain parish a new vicar was expected. The church was ancient, and was adorned with some curious wall paintings. The churchwardens considered the appearance of the building untidy and uncared for. So they set to work to whitewash the walls, obliterated the mural paintings, and even daubed the pulpit and font with their heedless brush. Far too many of these relics of ancient art have fallen victims to the ignorant custodians of our churches, or to the reforming zeal of the Puritan, who detected error in everything that was beautiful.

The practice of painting the walls of our churches dates as far back as Saxon times, but very few fragments of this pre-Norman art remain. That such existed is proved from the statement in the chronicle that Bishop Wilfrid of York decorated the capitals of the columns and the sacrarium arch of his church : " Historiis et imaginibus et variis celaturam figuris ex lapide prominentibus et picturarum et colorum grata varietate." The figures of saints on the splays of the windows at St. Mary's, Guildford, are probably Saxon work, and traces of this early colouring can be found at St. Nicholas Church, Ipswich, Britford Church, St. Martin's, Canterbury, and in a few churches which retain their original consecration crosses.

Of Norman work we have numerous examples, and sometimes we find that the early specimens of the art have been painted over in later Gothic times, and larger figures have eclipsed the more minute work of previous ages. At the Church of St. Lawrence, Reading, no less than five distinct series of paintings were discovered executed one over another. Alas ! in the nineteenth century " restoration " of the church they were all destroyed. But much Norman work remains, and many of the paintings of this period surpass those of later times in their brightness and depth of colouring and in their good condition. Frequently the favourite mouldings, cable, zigzag, chevrons, interlacing, semicircular arches, scroll and foliage patterns, imitation hangings, appear in the paintings of these Norman artists. Decorative colouring was employed to embellish the arches, as at Norwich and Ely Cathedrals, the orders of doorways, the soffits of arches, the splays of windows, which were often ornamented with bands of red and yellow, as at Barfreston and Kempley and Canterbury Cathedral. The cathedral of St. Albans contains some of the best examples of Norman painting. Not many scenes or figures were depicted at this period ; at least few remain which are indisputably Norman. We find some representations of bishops, Agnus Dei, scenes from the life of our Lord, the Apostles, the last judgment, St. George, scenes from the history of St. Nicholas, St. John writing the Apocalypse. These were some of the favourite subjects. The student will find some remarkable Norman paintings at Westmeston, including the Agnus Dei, Adoration of the Magi, betrayal, scourging, descent from the Cross, our Lord in glory delivering the keys to St. Peter and the book to St. Paul. Hardham Church has the Saviour in majesty, the last judgment, scenes from our Lord's life, and St. George on horseback. Barfreston, Chaldon, Patcham, Pirford, the crypt of Canterbury Cathedral, Copford, Kempley, are some of the churches where you will find some of the best examples of the paintings of this period. The twelfth-century paintings at Chaldon, Surrey, show the ladder of salvation of the human soul and the road to heaven, St. Michael weighing souls, and some very realistic representations of the torments of the wicked.

During the reign of Henry III great progress

was made in the art. Travelling monks roamed the country, leaving behind them in many a village church traces of their skill in artistic decoration. Foreigners flocked to England, but their advent did not influence the style of the native artists, who clung to their own methods and style. Amongst the favourite subjects of the Early English period were the murder of St. Thomas of Canterbury, the lives of St. Catherine of Alexandria, St. Nicholas, St. Margaret, St. Edmund, the seven acts of mercy, and the wheel of fortune. Scenes from the life of our Lord continue to appear, usually in the place of highest honour, in the chancel, the lives of the saints occupying the walls of the nave. Of the former, good examples may be found at Easby, Chalgrove, Timworth, East Wickham, Preston (Sussex), Wiston (Suffolk), Headington, Winchester Cathedral, and Faversham. There are some examples of thirteenth-century paintings at Winchester, in the chapel of the Holy Sepulchre. The subjects are: Our Lord's descent into Hades and the Saviour appearing to Mary Magdalen after His resurrection. St. Albans has some remarkable paintings of the Crucifixion. Old Testament subjects were not omitted. We find the creation and fall of man at Easby, and King David at St. Thomas's Church, Newport, Isle of Wight. Very numerous are the representations of St. Thomas of Canterbury, whose murder by the emissaries of King

Henry II exercised a powerful effect on the minds of churchmen. You will find the subject portrayed in the churches of Hauxton, Bramley (Hampshire), Preston (Sussex), and St. Cross, Winchester. St. Catherine appears at Winchester and Preston, where also is St. Margaret. St. Edmund is painted after the fashion of St. Sebastian, pierced with arrows, the king and martyr having been slain by the Danes. The cathedrals of Lincoln, Salisbury, Winchester, and Oxford have good examples of thirteenth-century work. The early English architects were devoted to the use of colour, and covered the surfaces of their walls, their piers, monuments, arches, and even their west fronts with an abundance of decorative painting. They were also very careful to prepare the surface of the walls for their work, a practice which was somewhat neglected by their successors. Hence their work has lasted well and endured through many centuries, whereas the paintings of the fourteenth-century artists have in many cases crumbled away owing to the decay of the plaster.

In the fourteenth century the Doom was the usual decoration of the space over the chancel arch. Examples may be seen at Bedfont, West Somerton, North and South Leigh, Alfriston, etc. There are over a hundred churches in this country containing representations of this subject, showing with much realism St. Michael weighing souls, the good being transported to a place of everlasting bliss, the evil being carried away by demons to endure the terrors of the fire that never shall be quenched. In some instances the Blessed Virgin is shown interceding for the souls. The miracles of our Lord appear at Warblington, and other events in our Lord's life are depicted at West Somerton, Crostwight, Islip, Bedfont, Plumpton, and many other places. Among the saints depicted at this period are St. Wulstan, St. Edward the Confessor, St. Erasmus, St. Martin, St. Faith, St. Edmund, St. Anthony, St. Sebastian, St. Christopher, St. Citha, St. Lawrence, and many others. Catfield Church had a remarkable set of paintings, now all covered with whitewash, representing scenes from the life of St. John Baptist, St. John the Evangelist, the martyrdom of SS. Lawrence and Katherine, the wheel of fortune, the seven deadly sins, the seven acts of mercy, and the seven sacraments. A very interesting fourteenth-century painting appears on the east wall of the chapter house at Westminster Abbey, where you can see a representation of the Blessed Trinity with seraphim and cherubim. This painting was the work of one John of Northampton. The small church at Little Kimble, Buckinghamshire, was completely covered with wall paintings. The best preserved figure is that of St. George, the style of whose armour gives the key to the date of the painting, which is about 1310. He has complete chain mail with round knee-caps of leather. Over

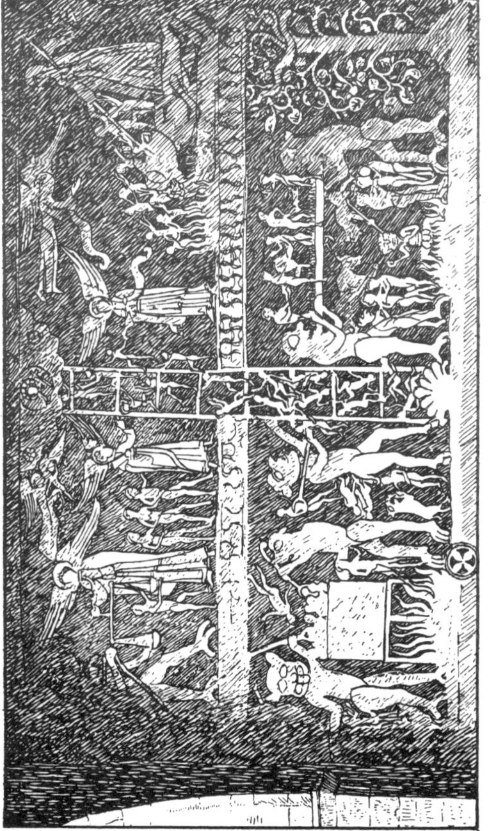

WALL PAINTING, CHALDON CHURCH, SURREY

the armour is a white surcoat with a red cross, which formerly bore a running pattern, dark brown on the paler red. The little shield bears the same cross, and the " gige " or strap for hanging it round the neck is twisted round the wrist. On either shoulder are " aiguilettes " which protect the head from a side cut. The long sword is worn slightly in front, and on the heels are " prick-spurs," the predecessors of the " rowel spurs." You can see the name " Georgius " in Longobardic characters. Many of the paintings are now almost perished. You can see the faint image of our Lord in a dark red garment, small outline figures representing souls in torment, a bishop wearing a red chasuble and holding a pastoral staff, and the head of a female saint ; two women, one apparently a nun holding a book, St. Francis preaching to the birds, the only example in England, the burial of St. Catherine, and a life-sized figure of an old man wearing a cowl and holding a book. Such are some of the remark-able examples which this little church affords, wrought " in the days of faith when patient thought brooded on things of God and doubted not." Faversham Church has several examples of paint-ings of the thirteenth and fourteenth centuries.

It would take far too large a space to record all the examples of the paintings of this period, and the reader is referred to the excellent *List of Buildings in Great Britain and Ireland having*

N

mural and other painted decorations of date prior to the latter part of the sixteenth century, compiled by Mr. Charles E. Keyser, M.A., F.S.A., and published by the Science and Art Department of the Committee of the Council on Education, South Kensington Museum. To this work the writer is indebted for much valuable information. Before leaving this brief description of the excellent work of the fourteenth-century artists, we should notice that the style of the designs closely follows the work of the builders and sculptors of the Decorated period. The stiff-leaved foliage and conventional flowers of the thirteenth century give place to more elaborate conceptions of artistic treatment, wherein Nature is followed more closely.

In the Perpendicular period the artists paid little attention to the work of their predecessors and frequently painted new designs over the earlier mural decorations. Paintings of this period are far more numerous than those of any other, and would require a far more extended space for their description than can here be accorded. We see the walls covered with diapers, shields, running scrolls with foliage and birds, pomegranates, and other varieties of ornamentation, besides the pictorial subjects. Diapers of the sacred monogram, of crowned " M's," the initial of the Virgin, often occur. There seems to have been a growing veneration for St. Christopher and St. George. The former usually has a staff, and is represented crossing a river, bearing the heavenly Child upon his shoulder. Strange-looking fish swim about his feet. On one side of the stream is a hermitage, with the figure of a hermit holding a lantern to guide the saint, and on the other side is a windmill. The figure of the saint is usually nearly life size, and often appears on the wall opposite the principal entrance, as it was deemed lucky to see St. Christopher on first entering a church. Moreover, the sight of the saint was deemed a preservation against violent death during the day, and also a prevention against drowsiness during the service, as the following verses show :—

> Christophori sancti speciem quicunque tuetur
> Illo namque die nullo languore tenetur.

Some churchwardens' accounts record the painting of the saint, as at St. Lawrence's Church, Reading, where the following item appears :—

" 1503-4. It. payd to Mylys paynter for painting of Seynt X°fer, viiis. iiij*d*."

He seems to have been regarded with much reverence by all classes. There are no less than eighty examples in Mr. Keyser's catalogue. There is a fine but faded one at Raunds, Northamptonshire. The dress of the Christ child and of the saint is a brown madder colour, and brown ochre is the colour of the sapling staff and the rocks, round which a large serpent is creeping.

The same church has a bold and spirited drawing

of St. George and the Dragon. He is clad in armour of the time of Edward IV, and wears a white surcoat with red stripes and belt. He has the long, pointed tippet hanging from his sleeve, fashionable in the reign of the Yorkist monarch. There is also a painting of the trial of St. Catherine, but it is a little doubtful whether it be the saint of Sienna or Alexandria, and another of her entombment. The murder of St. Thomas of Canterbury is also shown ; the archbishop is kneeling and is surrounded by a number of men with drawn swords and by cowled monks. On this wall above the chancel arch is a large painting representing adoring angels, each one bearing an instrument of the Passion. This forms a background to the rood. The ground is deep red, thickly studded with small black plates on which the sacred monogram is painted in white letters. The flowing robes of the angels and their wings are also white. The same church affords two examples of the Moralities which found much favour with the artists of the fifteenth and early sixteenth centuries. The vanity of human greatness is taught by the morality, " Les trois rois morts et les trois rois vifs," representing three kings going gaily hunting meeting three skeletons, the remains of kings once as powerful as they. In this example at Raunds, the three living monarchs are very gorgeously dressed, with their crowns and close-fitting tunics and red hoods and green or brown cloaks, carrying bouquets, all looking very fine and grand, a great contrast to the grinning skeletons of the deceased kings, who greet them with satirical gestures. Another morality is styled the purging of the Seven Deadly Sins. A spectre is shown spearing a finely dressed female, from whose sides emerge seven demons, each one devouring one of the deadly sins, anger, envy, sloth, avarice, pride, gluttony, and lechery. It would require much space in order fully to describe these admirable paintings, which are fast fading away.

South Leigh Church, Oxfordshire, has a remarkable series of paintings, of which we give some illustrations. Over the chancel arch is a Doom, on the north side are the saved, on the south the lost. The archangel, who descends to summon the saved, is clothed in white. Among the eighteen figures rising from their graves are a king and queen, a pope, a bishop, a monk, and a merchant. Above them is a scroll inscribed *Venite, Benedicti Patris mei.* Above the lost, who include a king, a queen, a nobleman, a monk, and a bishop, are the words *Discedite maledicti.* This painting is early fifteenth-century work. Of the same date is the painting of St. Michael weighing souls, the Virgin interceding. The figures of St. Clement and the Virgin with their emblems are late fifteenth-century work.

The wall paintings of England have suffered

greatly from various causes. They were regarded as relics of superstition by the iconoclastic Puritans. Little was done to destroy them until the reign of Queen Elizabeth, when at least some orders were issued to paint over " pictures and other like fancies " with sentences from Holy Scripture. But all wall painting did not cease, and several examples might be given of seventeenth-century art, including a representation of the destruction of the Spanish Armada at Bartoft. Not until the triumph of the Commonwealth were they doomed to destruction. The fanaticism of the Puritans revelled in the obliteration of these ancient works of art. Many of them were effectually hidden under various coats of whitewash and plaster, and after being long hidden have been brought to light again by the careful removal of the super-imposed surface by diligent and careful anti-quaries. Restoration and the ignorance of ancient art have sometimes again hidden them ; but we are learning better things now, and whenever an old mural painting is discovered, it is usually treated with proper respect, repaired, and restored when necessary, and preserved as a faithful memorial of bygone ages. Besides mural paint-ings our churches possess many good pictures by English artists and some copies of old Masters set up over the altar. A picture of the Last Supper by Sir James Thornhill is in Melcombe, Dorset ; Westall's " Joseph of Arimathea " at Eccleston,

Cheshire ; " Christ bearing His Cross," said to be by Luca Giordano, at Merton, Surrey. Copies of old Masters are in Honiton Church, Godshill, Selborne, Ellingham. Hideous figures of Moses and Aaron were sometimes set up in the eighteenth century. Many churches contain the Tables of the Commandments painted on boards, and texts in old English lettering and the royal arms, painted and gilded, appear in a large number of our ecclesiastical buildings.

CHAPTER XIV

PULPITS

"THE country parson preacheth constantly : the pulpit is his joy and his throne." So wrote the saintly George Herbert in the early years of the seventeenth century, when pulpits began to multiply in England, and those quaint and curious Jacobean structures arose and astonished the eyes of the rustics unaccustomed to such things. It must not, however, be supposed, although mediaeval pulpits are comparatively rare, that, therefore, the duty of preaching was neglected in pre-Reformation times. There is abundant evidence to the contrary. Chaucer's " poure parson of a town " used certainly to instruct his people.

> He was also a learned man, a clerk
> That Christe's Gospel trewely wolde preche,
> His parishens devoutly wolde he teche.
> But Christe's lore and His Apostles twelve
> He taughte, but first he followed it himselve.

Sermons were, perhaps, not so frequent as they are now. In the thirteenth century every priest was ordered to instruct his people four times a year in the vernacular, explaining the Creed, the Ten Commandments, the evangelical precepts, and other sacred truths. Elsewhere we find orders issued for this to be done every Sunday and holiday. Moreover, books were issued for the guidance of the preachers, and at visitations the sidesmen or synod's-men were asked whether their clergyman gave them proper instruction, and some amusing answers were received, showing that the rustic of the fifteenth century was not unlike his modern descendant in posing as a severe critic of his rector's sermons. Piers Ploughman also, in 1315, tells of preaching in a pulpit when he sings :—

> He is an heretick
> And yvele byleveth
> And precheth it in pulpit
> To blinded the people.

But we are concerned more with the parson's "joy and throne," as Herbert calls the pulpit, rather than with his discourses. The ambos, or ambones, were the earliest pulpits. Where there was no ambo the priest probably preached from the steps of the altar. That must have been the usual practice of the English Church prior to the erection of rood-lofts and screens. Indeed, it is doubtful whether ambos were universally used for preaching. The rising steps of the altar seem to have been the usual place for the delivery of sermons. Valerius shows that this was the custom in France till the time of Childebert. St. Augustine states that he was accustomed to preach from the exedra or apse of the church. Chrysostom, " the golden mouthed," on the other hand, is stated by Socrates and Sozomen to have preached from the ambo for the convenience of the multitude that assembled to hear him ; but these writers seem to declare that this custom was unusual.

When rood-screens were erected, naturally the chancel was somewhat shut off from the nave, and the altar step was not so convenient a place for the delivery of sermons. The intervention of the rood-loft and screen would impede the hearing of the words of the preacher as well as the view. In some of the larger Norman cross-shaped churches with a heavy central tower, even without a rood-screen it is difficult for the congregation in the nave to hear the priest ministering at the altar, and this difficulty would be greatly increased by the erection of the loft and screen, which was often a heavy structure of oaken timber framing. Hence the priest was obliged to draw nearer to the people. In mediæval documents the rood-loft is called the *pulpitum*. Thus Hugo, Abbot of St. Augustine's, Canterbury, wrote at the beginning of the twelfth century, *Pulpitum eciam in ecclesia fecit*, and it is usually supposed that the priest stood in it to read the Epistle and Gospel, and sometimes for the delivery of sermons.

It is, however, doubtful whether this was the usual practice in parish churches. In cathedrals and monastic churches it was customary " to erect two screens, the pulpitum, a fairly solid structure at the western boundary of the quire, and the rood-screen with the rood and loft to the westward of the pulpitum. At High Mass on great Feasts the Epistle and Gospel were solemnly sung from the pulpitum." [1]   But it is extremely improbable that this was done in ordinary parish churches, and much more so that they were used for preaching. The practical difficulties in the way of lofts ever having come into use generally for preaching are enormous, and, as Dr. Gasquet thinks, there must have been some form of pulpit, " an unpretentious wooden erection, perhaps in the screen or at the chancel arch," [2] whence the parson instructed his flock. Sometimes they may have been movable, as in the Roman Catholic Church of St. Mary of the Assumption, Aberdeen.[3]   In the fifteenth century there seems to have been an increased attention devoted to preaching, and many pulpits were erected, some of which have survived and will be hereafter described.

Among the ancient pulpits which have survived none are more interesting than those which were

[1] Aymer Vallance, F.S.A., on " Mediaeval Rood-lofts and Screens in Kent," in *The Memorials of Old Kent*, edited by P. H. Ditchfield and G. Clinch, p. 103.

[2] *Mediaeval Parish Life*, by Dr. Gasquet, p. 211.

[3] *Glossary of Liturgical Terms*, by Dr. Lee, p. 302.

erected in the refectories of monasteries. These were not for preaching, but for the reader, to read to the monks during mealtime, passages from holy Scriptures, homilies, some vivid chapters from the *Acta Sanctorum* or other godly tome, while they silently ate their dinners. The most perfect of these monastic pulpits is that of the beautiful Abbey of Beaulieu, in Hampshire, the refectory of which is now the parish church. It is of the latest Early English or earliest Decorated period, fashioned of stone, with a long flight of steps leading to it in the hollow interior of the wall. The panels are rich, with delicate flower tracery. Another similar pulpit exists at Chester, in the refectory of the Abbey of St. Werburga, which is now the cathedral. This pulpit is Early English work, a few years earlier than that at Beaulieu, and is approached by a similar flight of steps in the thickness of the wall. The staircase is open to the refectory by a trefoil-headed arcade of five bays of most graceful design ; and above each cluster of shafts is a quatrefoil opening, affording additional light to the staircase. At one time this refectory was used as a schoolroom for the boys of the king's grammar school, and this pulpit was covered with whitewash. Happily this disfigurement has been removed.

Another refectory pulpit exists at Shrewsbury, which stands solitary, bereft of its hall that once echoed with the sound of its reader's voice, and

alone points out the position of the monks'
chambers, which time and spoliation have
destroyed. This pulpit is a little gem of fourteenth-century architecture, and it is a sad pity
that the beautiful details should be exposed to
the weather in the incongruous surroundings of
a coalyard. It ought to be placed in a glass
case and preserved with reverent care. It is
octagonal. The three sides that faced the refectory were open ; the three opposite sides facing
the cloister were filled with glass. In one of
the remaining sides was the entrance, the steps
leading to it being in the thickness of the wall ;
and the opposite side was blank. The openings
on the side facing the refectory are filled, about
one-third of their height, with stone panelling,
each compartment containing two figures under
canopies. In the central panel there are figures
of the Angel Gabriel and the Blessed Virgin, signifying the Annunciation ; on the left of this centre
are the figures of SS. Peter and Paul, to whom
the monastery was dedicated, and on the right
side are those of St. Margaret and St. Bruno.
All these figures are much mutilated. The pulpit
has a groined roof, and the boss in the centre
is a beautifully carved representation of the Crucifixion. I believe these examples are all that remain
of the monastic refectory pulpits.

Another class of pulpit is the outdoor variety,
a form which has been found suitable to the needs

of modern times, an outdoor pulpit having been recently erected in the churchyard of St. James's Church, Piccadilly, London. The mediaeval preachers found them useful, and the most famous example remaining is that at Magdalen College, Oxford. Formerly there was a very remarkable one at St. Paul's Cross, London, where the Lord Mayor attended in state, and kings and queens came to hear the preachers.

As I have said, the fifteenth century was an age of preaching, and several pulpits date from that period. Very early in that century was erected the fine example in the grand church of St. Michael, Coventry. It has now disappeared, and its place is occupied by a handsome modern pulpit. Its date was about 1400 A.D. It was hexagonal, made of wood, mounted on a single somewhat slender stem, and it had a canopy or sounding-board coeval with the structure. Each side was divided into two panels with richly decorated canopies. It is impossible within the space of a short chapter to describe the many mediaeval pulpits which still remain in our parish churches. So-called " restoration " has removed a goodly number, and their place has been supplied by inartistic modern work. For example, in Parker's *Ecclesiastical Topography of England* (1850) there is a description of " a curious small stone pulpit projecting from the wall with the entrance behind " in his account of the charming

Berkshire church at Childrey. It has been since " restored " away. How many of the old pulpits have shared the same fate ! There is a sixteenth-century example at Wells, erected by Bishop Knight in the time of Henry VIII, a somewhat low but well-proportioned structure, resting on a basement, and fronted with panelled pilasters. The bishop's arms appear on it, and on the frieze is the inscription :—

Preache. thov. the. worde. be. fervent. in. season.
and. out. of. season. reprove. rebuke. exhorte.
wt. all longe. sufferyng. et. doctryne. 2 Timo.

There are a few Jacobean pulpits in our cathedrals, notably the fine one at Oxford, with its quaint grotesques, but most of the cathedral pulpits are modern.

Of the fifteenth-century pulpits I may mention the wooden structure in St. Mary's Church, Wendon, Essex, erected about 1440 A.D. ; the similar example at Fotheringhay, Northamptonshire, fashioned a few years earlier, with its remarkably handsome canopy, which has fan tracery in its roof and the royal arms at the back. The example at Nailsea Church, Somerset (*circa* 1500 A.D.), is interesting, especially in the arrangement of the staircase, which branches off from that which led to the rood-loft.

Some of the old pulpits were painted and gilded, and some, especially in Norfolk, have paintings of saints upon them, the favourite subjects being the four doctors of the Church— SS. Augustine, Ambrose, Gregory, and Jerome.

During the reigns of the later Tudors ecclesiastical affairs were unsettled and few pulpits were erected. With the advent of James I matters changed. The canons of 1603 ordered the churchwardens to provide in every church " a comely and decent pulpit, to be set in a convenient place within the same for the preaching of God's Word." Hence an enormous number of our churches have pulpits of this period, fantastically carved, and embellished with circular-arched panels, flat and shallow scrollwork, with huge sounding-boards over them. They were set in the north-east or south-east angles of the nave. The date of the pulpit is usually carved upon it. Take Berkshire as an example of the other counties. Nearly all the old pulpits are Jacobean, and many have escaped destruction in spite of " restoration." They were not deemed to be complete without a cushion, and several churchwardens were prosecuted for not providing this necessary equipment. Sometimes these cushions were fashioned out of beautiful old vestments. There was one at East Langdon Church, near Dover, of thick crimson silk richly embroidered with sprigs, and having two figures worked on it which were supposed to represent the Annunciation.

Another important accessory was the hour-glass,

to which our poets from Shakespeare to Long-fellow often make allusion. Churchwardens' accounts frequently refer to their erection. Thus in the accounts of St. Katherine's Church, Aldgate, London, we find the following entry :—

" Paid for an hour-glass that hangeth by the pulpit when the preacher doth make a long sermon, that he may know how the hour passeth away, one shilling."

The hour-glass did not always stay the Puritan's oratory, and many instances are recorded of the hour-glass being turned, and a second or even a third glass of eloquence being indulged in before a weary and starved congregation was permitted to retire homewards. Several of these hour-glasses remain, or rather the framework that held them. In two parishes adjoining my own they still exist. The pulpit at Hurst, Berkshire, in which Arch-bishop Laud certainly preached on two or three occasions, has a fine example. The bracket which supports the glass is a curious piece of ironwork, ornamented with the lion and unicorn and leaves and pomegranates. The letters E. A. (Elizabeth Armour) and the date 1636 appear, and a small iron plate is inscribed " As this glasse runneth, so man's life passethe." At Binfield, Berkshire, there is also a very fine pulpit, though mutilated. It bears the date " Ano. Dom. 1628," and has an elaborate hour-glass stand of hammered ironwork, consisting of oak-leaves and acorns, alternately

o

with vine-leaves and bunches of grapes, together with the arms of the Smiths' and Farriers' Company of London. The massive sounding-board has been relegated to the vestry.

There is a good Jacobean pulpit at Maisemore, Gloucestershire, with its hour-glass. On an inner panel is carved in high relief a design with the initials G. H., W. L., and the date 1636. The hour-glass is not in its proper position, and was placed there by the present vicar.

At Swaffham, Norfolk, there is a stout wrought-iron hour-glass bracket, and another at South Burlingham, in the same county, is attached to a fine fifteenth-century pulpit, which is enriched with stars, flowers, and tracery. The glass also remains. The Little Gidding example is fashioned in the form of irregular scrollwork, and the stand is in the form of a crown. An hour-glass stand at Hemsby, Norfolk, has been utilized for the purpose of holding a candle, and dethroned from its rightful position.

The tendency of Puritan teaching was to exalt the expounding of the Word of God above the sacramental teaching of the Church, and to make the hearing of sermons the chief means of grace. This opinion at once found expression in the arrangement of our churches. The Puritan was not content with his small Jacobean pulpit placed on one side of the chancel arch. He must have a great ponderous structure with pulpit soaring

JACOBEAN PULPIT AT MAISMORE, GLOUCESTERSHIRE

up aloft, with reader's desk below, and the clerk's desk another step beneath, erected in the centre of the church, blocking the view of the altar, and asserting itself with hideous pertinacity. This "three-decker," as it was sarcastically called, this "trireme" of monstrous proportions, reared its ugly head on high and utterly disfigured the church, converting it into a kind of conventicle and destroying all the ancient beauty and traditional teaching of the sanctuary. Happily a better day dawned and banished the "three-decker" to the shades and restored the church to its ancient glories and primitive beauty. Pulpits were relegated to their former position, the view of the altar was again revealed, and this alteration in the arrangement of our churches is symbolical of the teaching that Holy Communion is the highest act of Christian worship, and that though the preacher's words are winged by the Holy Spirit to the hearts of men and his duty a divine ordinance, the sermon may not take precedence of the sacraments, the chief means of grace to men.

CHAPTER XV

CHURCH PLATE

IN many of our churches there is some good
Church plate for the celebration of Holy
Communion. This store of treasure has been
often plundered, and it is wonderful that any
ancient pieces have been allowed to remain. The
Commissioners of Henry VIII and Edward VI took
away with them many beautiful chalices and patens
and other *instrumenta* with which many churches
both in town and country were endowed. Churchwardens and vicars, in order to prevent these
objects falling into the hands of these robbers,
sold many, and applied the proceeds to the repair
of the church, or of the roads, or to other purposes
for the cost of which they were liable. There
seems to have been a large amount of private
peculation in addition to public robbery for the
king's use. In Hertfordshire we read in the
returns of the Commissioners who were appointed
to discover missing articles that at Wormley one
Richard Houghton was accused of " embessilling
away " a chalice ; at Baldock two silver candlesticks had been taken by the late parson. Amongst

other missing goods that had been " embessillede " were a cross, candlesticks, silver chalice, vestments, a pax of silver, etc., the chief sinners being lords and knights, as well as parsons, parishioners, and churchwardens. The Commissioners were told to collect and bring together " all singular redye money, plate and juelles " and to confiscate them to the king's use. In order to prevent the loss of these valuables to the parish, the parochial authorities did not scruple to forestall the robbers and benefit the village, and perhaps themselves also, by appropriating and selling the goods.

We might contrast the inventory of church goods as made by the Commission with the list of treasure now in any church. Take, for example, the small village church of Boxford, in Berkshire, and note the valuables with which many generations of churchpeople had enriched it. There were in this church in the time of Edward VI the following :—

One chalice, a cross of copper and gilt, another cross of timber covered with brass, a cope of blue velvet embroidered with images of angels, one vestment of the same suit with an alb of Lockeram (a fine linen cloth), two vestments of Dornexe (stuff from Tournay or Dorneck), and three other very old, two old and coarse albs of Lockeram, two old copes of Dornexe, four altar cloths of linen cloth, two corporasses with cases whereof one is embroidered, two surplices and one rochett, one Bible and the paraphrases of Erasmus in English ; seven banners of Lockeram and one streamer, all painted ; three front cloths for altars, whereof one of them had paintings of white damask and black satin and the other two of old vestments ; two towels of linen, four candlesticks of latten and two standards (large candlesticks) before the high altar of latten ; a Lent veil before the high altar with panes blue and white ; two candlesticks of latten and five branches; a peace (pax) ; three great bells with one saunce or sanctus bell ; one canopy of cloth, a covering of Dornexe for the sepulchre (Easter sepulchre), two cruets of pewter, a holy-water pot of latten, a linen cloth to draw before the rood.

Such was the store of goods in an ordinary village church ere sacrilegious hands had fallen upon them. Most of the small churches in the same county had two chalices of silver and gilt. Englefield had a ship of brass, and many other objects and vestments are mentioned in these interesting inventories.[1] Nearly all have vanished. Some curious and valuable pieces of plate have remained to recent times. Unfortunately, the lust of the private collector has been excited and has been ministered to by dealers and silversmiths. A clergyman finds an old chalice which is rather worn and thin. He takes it to a jeweller to be

---

[1] *Parish Church Goods in Berkshire*, by Walter Money, F.S.A., 1879.

repaired, who tells him that it is hardly worth repairing, and offers the ignorant and unsuspicious parson a beautiful new set of vessels in return for the old chalice. The offer is accepted, and the tradesman sends the cup to Christie's or sells it to a collector, who gives a goodly sum of money, far exceeding the modest cost of the new plate which he has so generously presented to the clergyman. That little comedy or tragedy has been enacted in many parishes, and the sacred vessels have passed into the possession of gentlemen who love to exhibit their collections of old silver on their sideboards and dinner-tables ; and next to a cup won at racing you will see a chalice, and are reminded of Belshazzar's feast and the desecration of holy things for centuries used in the highest service of the Christian Church, and meditate upon the degeneracy of the times.

You will like to know something of the history of the plate that remains in your church. The oldest plate now existing has been found in tombs. It was the practice in former days to place a small chalice and paten in the coffin of an ecclesiastic as a symbol of his office. This was done in Saxon times, as in a Saxon cemetery at Reading a small metal chalice was discovered in the grave of a Saxon priest. This practice was continued in later times. At Nassington Church, Northants, in a grave in the north aisle was found the skeleton of a man who, as evinced by the presence of three escallops or palmer's shells, had performed a pilgrimage to the Holy Land, and with the skeleton there were a small pewter chalice and paten.[1] The former has a bell-shaped bowl with slight lip, the stem slender and cylindrical with knot in the centre, and the foot circular ; the paten has a single circular depression with rather broad edge. This is of the earliest type, and may be assigned to the middle of the thirteenth century. An early chalice and paten were found at Sandford, Oxfordshire, which belong to the beginning of the fourteenth century. The bowl is broader and shallower and lacks the lip. The earliest post-Conquest chalice in existence, actually used in the church of Berwick St. James, Wilts, until a few years ago, is now in the British Museum. It is parcel gilt. Its bowl is broad and shallow, the stem and knot, by which the vessel was held, and the foot being plain and circular. From 1250 to 1275 the makers fashioned the stem and knot separately from the bowl and foot, and shaped them polygonally, the foot being circular. During the remaining years of that century the foot was worked into ornate lobes, which radiate from the stem over the surface of the foot. Then from 1300 to 1350 the bowl was deepened and made more conical. At the end of that period the custom arose of

[1] *Journal of the Society of Architects :* " Church Plate," by Christopher A. Markham, F.S.A. New Series, vol. vii., No. 73, p. 7.

laying the chalice on its side on the paten to drain the ablutions at Mass ; and as the round-footed chalices would have a tendency to roll, the foot was made hexagonal for the sake of stability. Henceforth all the mediaeval chalices were fashioned with a six-sided foot. By degrees the bowl became broader and shallower, and instead of the base having six points, its form is a sexfoil without any points. During the later half of the fifteenth century the stem took to itself six sides and became longer than it was before, and was sometimes covered with tracery, having buttresses at the angles. The knot is ornamented with angels' heads, flowers, and other designs ; the foot is plainer and flatter than in the previous periods, and in one of the compartments of the base there is a representation of a crucifix or the Virgin or ihc or xpc.

In the last period of pre-Reformation times the bowl is broad and shallow and reverts almost to the shape of the early hemispherical form, and the stem and knot are more ornate than in the previous examples. Some of these early chalices bear the inscription :—

Calicem salutaris accipiam et nomen Domini invocabo.

Patens, also, have been classified and approximate dates assigned to them according to the shape and number of the depressions in their surface. They bear devices, such as the *Manus*

Dei, or hand of God, in the act of blessing ; on later ones the vernicle or face of our Lord, the Holy Trinity, the Agnus Dei, the sacred monogram. The oldest paten is said to be that found at Chichester Cathedral in a coffin, and its date is about the year 1180. In the centre is a rude engraving of the Agnus Dei, and it bears the inscription :—

✠ Agnus Dei qui tollis pecata mundi miserere nobis.

The grave of Bishop Grosteste, at Lincoln, yielded up an ancient paten (1230-53), which has the figure of a bishop vested, the right hand raised in the act of blessing, the left holding a pastoral staff. The oldest piece of Church plate still in use is a remarkable paten at Wyke Church, near Winchester, the date of which is about 1280. It bears an engraving of the Agnus Dei holding a banner, and round the rim is the legend :—

✠ Cuncta : creo : virtute : rego : pietate reformo.

Another favourite inscription was *Benedicamus patrem et filium cum spiritu sancto;* but on the paten in the church of Great Waltham, Essex, the important word *spiritu* is omitted for want of space.

I am afraid that it is unlikely that your church should possess any of this pre-Reformation plate, as the examples left to us are not numerous. According to two of the great authorities on this subject, Messrs. W. H. St. John Hope and T. H. Fallow, only thirty-eight chalices and eighty-four patens have survived the pillaging of our churches in the time of Henry VIII and Edward VI. But these were not the only forms of plate that existed in our churches in mediaeval times, and before we pass on to the changes wrought after the Reformation it may be well to search for other treasures which our churches contained.

Every church had its censer or thurible which was used for incense, which formed a part of mediaeval ritual and is not unknown in our churches to-day, in spite of episcopal censure and various judgments. Objections to its use do not seem to be serious. It formed part of the Jewish ceremonial service, and has a beautiful symbolical meaning. As the clouds of incense arise to the roof of the church, so the prayers of the faithful ascend to the throne of God. In the religious ceremony of consecrating a lodge of Freemasons incense plays its part, and often the strictest Protestants, who would hasten to condemn its use in church, find no objection or fault with it in the mysterious secret recesses of the craft. In our old parish churches censers were made of gold or silver or silver gilt, more usually of brass or latten, and were shaped in the form of a covered vase or cup, perforated so as to allow the fumes of burning incense to escape. Sometimes the incense vessel is fashioned in the form of a ship, and is often of a very interesting design. Many examples of censers are preserved in the South Kensington Museum, the British Museum, and in private collections. In the private chapels of Roman Catholic families there are some of ancient date, at Buckland and East Hendred House, Berkshire, and at Stonor Park, near Henley-on-Thames. Sometimes the top of the vessel is shaped like the tower or spire of a church, and occasionally like a shrine. Lord Carysfort has a very fine silver gilt censer that was evidently thrown into Whittlesea Mere by the monks of Ramsay Abbey in order to prevent it from falling into the hands of the Commissioners. It remained there until recent times, when the lake was drained and the vessel recovered. In Dr. Cox's *Church Furniture* several discoveries of ancient censers are recorded in the churches wherein they are preserved. Poynings Church, Sussex, has a wooden one, which is used as an alms-dish.

Old inventories always mention a pyx, a box or vessel of gold or silver, in which the Host was reserved for the sick and infirm. It often resembles a chalice, except that instead of the bowl there is a covered receptacle for the Host. I remember well the discovery of a beautiful specimen which was dug up in the churchyard of Yateley, Hampshire. The pyx was hung in front of the altar, covered by a pyx cloth in the form of a canopy or veil. This was made of rich materials—silk, satin, or cloth of gold—and was richly embroidered. A fine example of pyx cloth still exists at Hessett, in Suffolk.

Another important piece of mediaeval plate was the monstrance, in which the Blessed Sacrament was carried in procession and exposed on the altar. The form of the monstrances varied. Sometimes they were made in the shape of a tower or a covered chalice, sometimes in the form of images carrying silver pyxes, in which the Sacrament was placed, elaborately ornamented with many jewels. Another form was that of a circle surmounted by a cross, and placed on a stand like the stem and foot of a chalice. The Host was placed on a stand in the midst of the circle, which was surrounded by rays of glory. Processions were always a great feature of mediaeval worship ; hence the monstrance was frequently in use, especially on such occasions as the celebrations of Corpus Christi Day.

Holy oil was much used in the services. It was blessed by a bishop on Maundy Thursday, and used in Baptism, Confirmation, and Extreme Unction, as well as at the consecration of churches, ordination, and the coronation of kings. The vessel for holding the oil was an important piece of Church plate, and was called a chrismatory. Usually there were three distinct vessels, one for holding the oil for the sick, a second for the chrisma or balm used at confirmations, ordinations, and consecrations, and a third for the baptismal oil. Sometimes these vessels are labelled with the words EXT. UNC., CAT., and CHR., according to the recommendation of St. Charles Borromeo, in order that each oil might be kept for its proper use and that no confusion might arise. At New College, Oxford, there are the remains of an ancient chrismatory, wherein the compartments were distinguished by the letters O for *oleum*, C for *chrisma*, and V for *unctio*. Two other examples have been discovered, one at St. Martin's, Canterbury, and the other at Granborough, Buckinghamshire.

The pax was a small tablet of silver or other precious metal used for giving the kiss of peace during High Mass. The celebrant kissed the tablet, and held it aloft before all the people. It then seems to have been passed round by the clerk to each person in the congregation, who reverently kissed it. Its shape was usually oblong, and at the back of it there was a handle. It was usually adorned with a representation of the Agnus Dei, a crucifix with the usual attendant figures of the Virgin and St. John, the Nativity, the Blessed Virgin and Infant Jesus ; or the vernicle, or *vera icon*, a representation of our Lord's face miraculously delineated on the napkin of St. Veronica when He was being led to execution upon the cross.

The church plate included also two small cruets for containing the wine and water used in Holy Communion, one engraved with the letter V (*vinum*) and the other A (*aqua*), of which there are a few examples remaining ; also a sacring bell, often made of silver, which was rung during the service at the time of the elevation of the Host ; and most churches possessed a processional cross. A pathetic little gift occurs in the will of Edward Ball, of Barkham. He had seen the little church despoiled of its treasures and wished to restore some of these. He was probably the donor of a very handsome Elizabethan Communion cup, dated 1561, and in his will he directed that five shillings should be spent for the purchase of a cross to be carried before the choir at Barkham Church. Alas ! this no longer exists, and we should wish some equally pious donor to supply the place of this cross which Edward Ball, an ancestor of Mary Ball, the mother of General Washington, once gave to our little Barkham Church.

A clean sweep was made of most of these treasures which our churches contained at the Reformation. Henceforth the plate was confined to a chalice and paten, alms-dish and a large silver flagon, which we will proceed to describe. The form of the chalice was entirely changed. Prior to the Reformation the bowl of the chalice became smaller and shallower, on account of the gradually introduced practice of refusing the wine in Holy Communion to the laity. When they were restored to their primitive right and could again enjoy the privilege of which a strange development of doctrine and ritual had deprived them, a larger bowl was required, and also a much larger receptacle for the wine to be used in the Sacrament than the small cruets that sufficed in pre-Reformation times. Hence we have the introduction of capacious flagons, which many churches now possess.

Somewhere about the year 1562 some order seems to have been made with regard to the shape of these Communion cups,[1] inasmuch as all these Elizabethan chalices conform to the same sort of type, though they vary in details. Our Barkham cup may be taken as an example of this type, though it has no cover, as in many instances, which cover was used as a paten. It is made of silver, and the bowl is slightly bell-shaped, with

[1] The cup here at Barkham bears the date mark 1561, and is similar in shape to the usual Elizabethan type. So the order, which has never been found, may have been issued a little earlier. Mr. Markham declares in his paper on "Church Plate" in the *Journal of the Society of Architects* that we ought not to call this vessel used in Holy Communion a " chalice," and that " cup " is the correct term. I fail to follow his reasoning. It is true that in the Book of Common Prayer the word " cup " is used, though in the rubric in the Consecration Prayer the word chalice occurs ; but no argument can be derived from that. The altar is called the Lord's Table by the compilers of our Prayer Book, but it did not cease to be an altar ; nor did the chalice cease to be a chalice, though it was called a cup.

POST REFORMATION CHALICES WITH PATEN COVERS

1. SILVER PARCEL-GILT, DIGSWELL, HERTS (1563-4)
2. SILVER-GILT, RICKMANSWORTH, HERTS (EARLY 18TH CENTURY)
3. SILVER-GILT, ST. JAMES'S GARLICKHYTHE, LONDON (1549)

a stem and knob and circular base. Around the bowl at the top there is an engraved band of spiral ornament. It is a very charming example, which we prize very much. In some of the later Elizabethan chalices the knob disappeared. In Jacobean times a different pattern was introduced, and we have standing cups with covers which are no longer used as patens. The influence of Archbishop Laud is seen in the shape of chalices of Charles I's time, when they reverted to that of the mediaeval cups, having small conical bowls, tall hexagonal stems with knots and a six-pointed foot.

After the Restoration chalices assumed a heavier design, having capacious bowls, thick stems and plain feet. At the end of the seventeenth century and beginning of the eighteenth they were more elegant, and then the art languished and the Communion vessels lost all beauty of design and artistic workmanship, from which debased period we have now emerged.

In our Barkham Church we have an immense silver flagon, which is dated 1729, and was the gift of Dame Henrietta Kingsmill, of Sydmonton, Hampshire. These inscribed vessels are interesting, as they record the thankofferings of pious donors on the occasion of some great event in the national annals, or some private mercy vouchsafed to the individual. They record the connection of some family with the parish, the arms they bore, and the hallmarks tell us of their date, which is

P

often anterior to the date of the inscription. Pre-Reformation plate sometimes bears the names of donors, which are usually accompanied by a request that worshippers will pray for their souls.

Flagons replaced the small cruets which were in use in mediaeval times before the laymen were permitted to partake of the hallowed wine. In the sixteenth century they resembled somewhat in form the cruets they supplanted, but were of larger size ; in the seventeenth they assumed the tall tankard shape, which was maintained for a long period. Other articles sometimes found in the church plate chest are spoons for straining the wine and removing any foreign body that may have become mixed with it. Apostle spoons are favourite objects for collectors, and the figures upon them denote their former ecclesiastical use. There is an apostle spoon at Dallington, Northants, which was made at York in 1597, and another at Ramsbury, Wilts.

In order to determine the age of the plate in your church it is only necessary to obtain a copy of Mr. Cripps's *Old English Plate*. Therein you will find a list of the hallmarks. These were first introduced in 1300 by King Edward I in order to keep up the purity of silver, and consisted of the lion's or leopard's head crowned. This was the king's mark. The maker's mark was introduced in 1363, and was some initial or badge chosen by the silversmith. To these were added in 1438 the year letter or assayer's mark, a different letter being chosen for each year. When the alphabet was exhausted, another with different shaped letters was begun. In 1545 the lion passant was introduced, and since 1784 the portrait of the reigning monarch has appeared. With a list, therefore, of the alphabets used in marking plate, it is not very difficult to discover the date of any piece of silver.

Besides the plate that has been described, many of our humbler churches possess pewter vessels, of which there is a great store in all parts of England, and some that is still in use. In the parish of Arborfield there is a paten and flagon of pewter, which were formerly in the church, but are now kept at the Hall. In some churches, even at the present day, pewter vessels are used in the service of Holy Communion. This is, perhaps, excusable when the parishes are very poor, but will no generous churchman present some plate of purer metal for the celebration of the highest act of our religion?

In many out-of-the-way places valuable and interesting pieces of church plate have reposed unsuspected by the world outside the retired corner in which they are situate. They are no longer permitted to remain unseen and unknown save by the parson and his flock, who often know little of their value and importance. Inventories are being made in many counties and dioceses, and one of the many uses of the *Victoria County Histories*, which are nearing completion, will be to disclose the stores of church plate that many obscure churches possess. They should be cherished with a whole-hearted affection, not only on account of their sacred uses, but as interesting memorials of the bygone history of the parish and of the generous donors who gave them to the church they loved, under whose shade they rest.

CHAPTER XVI

MONUMENTAL EFFIGIES AND BRASSES

MANY memorials of the dead cluster round our churches. When we sit alone and meditate therein we seem to see the ghosts of countless generations of villagers haunting the place where in life they worshipped and which was associated with all the great events in their lives. Here is the grave of a monk. A sister-in-law of the writer, one afternoon when the evening shadows had begun to fall, actually saw the cowled figure of this monk kneeling in prayer just above his tomb. You may see strange sights. That sturdy Elizabethan knight dressed in armour lying beside his much-ruffed wife is coming to tell you of the stirring times in which he lived, of how he fought the Spaniard in the Armada, and wants to know what sort of folk the men of England are to-day, and whether they are ready to guard the fair isle which he and his companions fought so hard to defend. Here comes a parson with a Geneva cap hiding a tonsured head, who still wears an anxious face and wonders whether he was right to follow the example of his neighbour of Bray ; and another with stern look and determined mien who defied Cromwell and all his crew, was turned out of his benefice, endured the bitterest poverty, but lived to oust the Puritan minister who had ousted him, when the king enjoyed his own again. We read the fulsome adulation showered down upon some great lady on the tablet in the chancel that records her memory, and are unprepared to meet the sharp-tongued scold who even in ghost-life can make herself extremely unpleasant. They throng around us—these ghosts and memories, until the dead seem more real than the living, and lead us to a careful examination of their monuments and memorials.

In old churches we often find stone coffins, the space for the deceased person having been hollowed out of a block of stone with a head-shaped recess at one end for the head. This was covered with a lid composed of a stone slab, and the burial was made in the floor of the church, the lid forming part of the pavement. On this lid was often cut a single cross, and sometimes the relatives added a device which showed the trade, rank, or profession of the deceased. Thus a chalice and paten denoted a priest ; a sword showed a knight ; an axe, a forester; an inkhorn, a notary ; shears, a wool merchant. When the stone coffin was not placed in the floor of the church, the surface of the lid was raised in the centre and sloped to the sides. It was then more elaborately carved ; the cross assumed a much more decorated form. At Tickhill, in Yorkshire, there is a stone coffin-lid which is adorned with a cross that has a beautiful floriated head with the *Agnus Dei* in the centre.[1] Two strange beasts something like dragons are devouring the foliage, and a sword grasped by a hand denotes that the deceased was some knight or warrior, though his name has passed away.

Our forefathers evidently felt that they did not sufficiently honour the memory of the deceased by simply recording the symbol of their trade or profession, and at the beginning of the thirteenth century it occurred to some one to preserve the likeness of his departed friend as well as the devices that disclosed the rank and station in life. Moreover, he desired to preserve his friend's name. Hence he caused to be carved an inscription along the side of the lid, recording the name and achievements of the dead person, the date of the death, together with a pious prayer that God would have mercy on the soul of his dear friend. *Cujus anima propicietur Deus*, is a common form of prayer which was in early days expressed in Norman-French, and later on in homely English. Latin inscriptions usually begin, *Orate pro anima.* A common French one is as follows : " de quy alme tout puissant dieu eit m'ci, Amen."

[1] A figure of this fine coffin-lid is given in Mr. Clinch's *Old English Churches*, p. 183.

The early examples of sepulchral effigies at the beginning of the thirteenth century were carved flat upon the surface of the slabs ; but ere fifty years had passed away the art of the sculptor produced magnificent monumental effigies. In the early instances of flat effigies they sometimes carved the head and feet in low relief and left out the body part of the figure, sculpturing out on the centre of the slab the coat-of-arms of the deceased. From this primitive form were soon developed high tombs with recumbent statuesque effigies placed under ornamental canopies or arched recesses in the wall or enclosed within chantry chapels. Knights and nobles lie clad in armour with their ladies by their sides. Bishops and abbots bless the spectators with their uplifted right hands. Judges lie in their official garb, and merchants with the emblems of their trade. At their feet lie animals, a dog or a lion, or some creature that had some heraldic connection with the family of the deceased, or was symbolical of his work. Thus a merchant appropriately places his feet on a sheep or a woolpack which had brought to him his wealth ; a vintner upon two wine-casks. In some instances the figure of a dog at the foot of an effigy represents some favourite animal. There is a brass memorial of Lady Cassy at Deerhurst, in Gloucestershire, and this lady places her feet upon a dog, shown with his collar of bells and his name "Terri" attached. Similarly Sir Bryan Stapleton's dog "Jakke" used to appear on his brass at Ingham, Norfolk, until the vandals destroyed this memorial. He must have been a curious little dog, and I should be sorry to have to declare his breed, as "Jakke" had a sharp nose, a Pomeranian ruff, and a smooth body.

In examining these effigies we often notice knights and warriors represented with their legs crossed, and we are told that this denotes that they were Crusaders. Indeed, popular belief assures us that if the legs are crossed at the ankles the knight went to the Crusades once ; if at the knees, twice ; if at the thighs, three times. Even vergers at cathedrals, who are usually well-informed concerning the history of the buildings they so often describe, have gravely imparted to me this traditional view. Perhaps it is hardly worth while, when every one is interested in architecture and ecclesiastical antiquities, to contradict this popular superstition. It is known that many warriors who are so represented never went to the Crusades, and that others who have no cross-legged effigies did go to the Holy Wars. It was evidently the fashion and conceit of the sculptors of those days, and apparently had no particular significance.

Most of these figures in mediaeval times appear in a recumbent position, but not all. In Bakewell Church, Derbyshire, there is a remarkable monument, placed against one of the nave piers, in memory of Sir Godfrey Foljambe, who died in 1376, and Avena, his second wife, the co-founders of a chantry in that church. They are represented in half-length figures of alabaster, set erect, carved in high relief, beneath a double crocketed canopy. The knight wears plate armour, and has on his head a conical helmet with a camail of mail attached to its lower edge. The lady wears a reticulated head-dress or cowl. Over the knight are the arms of Foljambe, and over the lady those of Ireland, she having been the daughter and heir of Sir Thomas Ireland.[1] Another position is shown in the curious tomb of another member of the Foljambe family. It is a table tomb, on the sides of which are many sculptured figures of squires and ladies, represent-ing the seven sons and seven daughters of Henry Foljambe. On the top of the table are the renewed brass memorials of the deceased and his wife, and the figure of a knight kneeling at the foot of these brasses.[2]

Alabaster was a very favourite material for monuments in the Middle Ages. There are con-siderable deposits in Derbyshire and Staffordshire whence large blocks were quarried. The softness of this material enabled the sculptors to produce wonderful effects with comparative facility, and there are a very large number throughout the

[1] *Memorials of Old Derbyshire.* Edited by Dr. Cox, F.S.A., p. 108.
[2] *Ibid.*

country of alabaster monuments. The head of the effigy usually rests upon a cushion, and this is often supported by figures of angels.

Every county possesses these memorials of the dead. The Aldworth effigies are some of the most remarkable. In this out-of-the-way village church on the Berkshire downs there are the De la Beche monuments, nine in number, which were probably all erected at the same time in the fourteenth century. There are six knights in armour, five of whom are cross-legged, all of large stature (the villagers call them " the giants "), and beside these sleeping warriors there is a civilian and two ladies. The Decorated canopies under which six of them rest proclaim their age, and there are two table monuments between the pillars of the south arcade. One of the figures used to be under an arch on the outside of the church. Captain Symonds, who fought for the king in the Civil War, made some valuable antiquarian notes and recorded that " The common People call ye Statue under ye outside of ye Churche John Everafraid, and say further that he gave his foule to the Divil if ever he was buried either in Churche or Churchyard ; so he was buried under the Churche wall, under an Arche." The bricked-up arch is still there. Popular tradition has given the names of John Long, John Strong, and John Neverafraid to other giants. I should like to stop and tell you about these De la Beches, who figure in history ; one of them, Sir

Nicholas, was tutor to John of Gaunt ; another was keeper of the Tower of London, where the royal children were in his custody during the absence of the king in France ; and there was a mighty commotion when his majesty returned unexpectedly and found the knight absent from his duties. I should like, too, to identify the monuments. This has been done, but it is wholly conjectural, and we need not stay to try to solve that which is inscrutable.

The monuments at Aldworth are not the only instance of the descendant of some great family preserving the memory of his ancestors by erecting these gorgeous tombs. The Fettiplaces were an illustrious race, and their importance is recorded in the popular distich :—

> The Traces, the Lacys and the Fettiplaces
> Own all the manors, the parks and the chases.

In Swinbrook Church, Oxfordshire, one side of the chancel is occupied by ponderous monuments of the scions of the family, consisting of figures clad in armour lying on shelves and dating from the sixteenth century. In the church of Chester-le-Street there is a long series of monuments erected by John, Lord Lumley, in the same century, to his ancestors. I remember the sad story of some family of the *nouveaux riches* type calmly appropriating the monuments of an ancient race, but happily I cannot remember the scene of this gross vandalism.

There are few old churches which do not contain some of these monumental effigies of mediaeval times. An important section of them are the wooden effigies which my friend, Dr. Fryer, has investigated and described in *Archæologia*. He tramped some hundreds of miles in order to visit each example, and his peregrinations brought him to my village of Barkham, where we have in the church a wooden monument which we have identified as Dame Agnes Neville, who married one of the Bullocks of Arborfield. This lady was an heiress, and some of her land was unjustly seized by Mautravers, whose estates, on account of his treason, were confiscated by the king. She applied for the restitution of that which Mautravers had taken, and through the assistance of Thomas Bullock, the king's reeve, regained her land ; and Master Bullock, seeing that she was a great heiress, succeeded in arranging her marriage with his son. The poor lady's monument has been very badly treated, but we prize it as a memorial of an interesting personage.

At the beginning of the sixteenth century a different style of monument arose, which owed its origin to the employment of foreign craftsmen introduced by Henry VIII. These men brought with them classical ideas and methods of work which developed into what is now called the English Renaissance. The larger monuments of this class consist of a table tomb upon which lie the effigies of the man and his wife, and supported by marble columns is a heavy canopy, which shows classical Renaissance details embellished with arms and figures. The children of the deceased are usually represented by kneeling figures, the males on their sire's side, the girls near their mother. Later on the recumbent position of the figures was abandoned, and they are shown kneeling, often in mural monuments, one on each side of a prayer-desk. Later still they are carved in a sitting or standing posture, and the old idea of prayerful and religious contemplation is abandoned. This is also borne out by the inscriptions. No longer does the monument silently petition that God will have mercy on the soul of the deceased, but it sets forth in laudatory Latin his virtues, and the prowess of the epitaph-writer was taxed to produce fulsome compliments in English prose or rhyme enumerating the graces and perfections of the deceased.

Another form of effigy was commonly in use in pre-Reformation times, in addition to figures that have been described. These are called incised effigies, which were cut in outline upon flat slabs of stone, the lines being filled in with enamelled metals. Thornton Abbey, Lincolnshire, and Brading, in the Isle of Wight, have examples of this work. But the great expense of these enamels, and their frailty when exposed in the pavements of churches, led to the use of brass ; and hence arose the introduction of memorial brasses, for which England is famous.

The word brass is a misnomer. The substance of which these memorials are composed was called in olden times latten, and is made up of copper and zinc with a small admixture of tin and lead. It was manufactured in Flanders and Germany and sent into this country, and not until the mediaeval period had passed away was it produced in England, when its quality sadly deteriorated. Mr. Macklin, President of the Monumental Brass Society, has contributed a volume to the *Antiquary's Books* on the *Brasses of England*, and he divides the existing examples into the following periods :—

The first period covers the reigns of Edward I and Edward II, 1272-1327. The second from 1327-99, extending to the reign of Richard II. The third is the Lancastrian, from 1400 to 1453. The fourth is that of the Wars of the Roses, 1453-85. The fifth is the Tudor, from 1485 to 1558. The sixth begins with Elizabeth and extends to the extinction of the art in the eighteenth century. The periods are sometimes described as corresponding with the usual styles of architecture, Early English (thirteenth century), Decorated (fourteenth century), Perpendicular (fifteenth and part of the sixteenth centuries), and Renaissance ; but the chief authorities on the subject have adopted the former division.

The execution of almost all of our English brasses is due to native artists, and their work differs much from that which was produced abroad. Foreign brasses are usually of great size, and consist of a rectangular sheet of metal, on which is engraved the figure, under a canopy, the background being ornamented with rich diaper, foliage, and scrollwork, and the incisions filled with colouring. I tried to obtain a rubbing of one such brass in a Dutch church, but it is not necessary to go abroad to find examples of foreign manufacture. There are several in this country : at King's Lynn, Norfolk ; St. Albans Abbey; Wensley, Yorkshire; North Mimms, Hertfordshire ; Aveley, Essex; Newark, Notts ; Topcliffe, Yorkshire. All these are fourteenth-century work, and there are others of a later period at Newcastle, Ipswich, Fulham, All Hallows, Barking, and Aberdeen. At King's Lynn there is a brass erected to the memory of Robert Braunche and his two wives. He was mayor of the town in 1349. At the foot of these brasses is usually depicted some scene, and under the above example there is a representation of the peacock feast, which seems to have been a very splendid occasion, when musicians discoursed sweet music, a famous banquet was spread, and busy attendants served the guests seated at a long table. In most of these foreign brasses, besides the chief figures, there are prophets, saints and angels under splendid canopies, dragons, lions, or pet-dogs beneath the feet of the deceased, much ornamented background, and inscriptions in Lombardic characters.

There is no resemblance between these foreign brasses and those made by English artists. Those produced in this country consist of separate pieces with an irregular outline, corresponding to that of the figure. They have no brass background, and for delicacy of engraving and general appearance they are far the best. No other country can boast of so large a number as England, in spite of the hard usage they have received and of much wanton destruction. In most old churches you will see the matrices of brasses, i.e. the cut spaces on stone slabs which have been robbed of the metal, proclaiming the pillaging of our sanctuaries and the work of the nefarious hands of church robbers.

We will try to give some examples of the brasses of the various periods. There are some four thousand still remaining in England, so that our review can only be slight. Those who are interested in the subject are advised to refer to Mr. Macklin's book, or to Haines's *Brasses* and other kindred works. My friend, Mr. Mill Stephenson, F.S.A., is acquainted with every brass in the country. He is preparing a *magnum opus* on the subject, which, when it appears, will be the most exhaustive and valuable book on brasses that has ever been compiled.

Many years ago I stated in my book on *English Villages* that the oldest brass in the kingdom is

Q

that of Sir John D'Aubernown at Stoke Dabernon, Surrey, which was fashioned in 1277, and I am glad to find that no subsequent discovery has made that statement incorrect. The earliest of which we have any record is that of Simon de Beauchamp, at St. Paul's, Bedford, who died before 1208. It is mentioned by Leland, and the matrix remains, and there are traces of about six others, at Wells, Salisbury, Lynwode, and elsewhere ; but the D'Aubernown brass is the earliest existing one. The knight is clad in chain armour with a long linen surcoat open in front. He bears a shield on which appears his coat of arms, a sword and lance with fringed pennon, and wears single-pointed spurs.

It may be here noted that there is no more correct record of the history of armour and of costume than is contained in these brass memorials. You can trace the changes in the fashion and style of armour which took place between the thirteenth and seventeenth centuries, and also the picturesque costumes of ladies with their curious head-gear, and the no less various fashions of the male civilian's dress.

Another very early brass is that of Sir Richard de Boselyngthorpe, at Buslingthorpe, Lincolnshire, which is deemed to be dated about 1290. It is a small demi-figure set in a large stone slab surrounded by an inscription in Lombardic letters. He appears in chain mail, and wears gloves and a surcoat, and holds a heart in his hands. Other brasses of this period are those of Sir Roger de Trumpington, at Trumpington, near Cambridge (1289), Sir Robert de Bures, at Acton, Suffolk (1303) ; and there are about sixteen others. The earliest lady's brass is at Trotton, in Sussex (about 1310), which commemorates Margaret de Camoys. It has been robbed of some of its beauty ; the white spaces show the matrices of a canopy, and several small shields and stars which were probably enamelled. You will notice the veil and wimple and fillet across her brows and the little curls beneath it.

The earliest brasses of a priest are cross brasses at Chinnor, Oxfordshire, and Woodchurch, Kent, both of which are dated about 1320. The latter is to the memory of Nichol de Gore, who is clad in eucharistic vestments, and stands in a quatre-foiled circle bearing the inscription : "Mestre Nichol de Gore gist en ceste place Jhesu Crist prioms ore qe merci lui face." Fleurs-de-lis adorn the points of the cross.

We pass on to what Mr. Macklin calls the golden age of Plantagenet rule, the second and best period of English brass-work. Merchants and tradesmen have advanced in wealth and share the glories of a brazen memorial with knights and warriors, their ladies and ecclesiastics. Beautiful canopies sur-round the figures, and sometimes there is a border composed of a series of canopied niches, each con-taining the figure of a saint or warrior. The armour of knights has much changed. In the thirteenth century they wore helmet and hauberk of chain mail, the sleeves continued into gauntlets, the palms of which were free from rings in order to give a firmer grasp of sword or lance. The thighs were protected by haut-de-chausses, mailed only in the exposed parts and not on the seat, and the legs have chausses of chain mail. The surcoat is of a graceful fashion and was often embroidered with crosses or other devices, and secured by a narrow belt about the waist. The shield is triangular or heater-shaped. The sword is long, straight, and double-edged with a cross-guard.

The effigies of the fourteenth century show many changes in this knightly equipment, which we can observe very closely by comparing the figures, until at length it is developed into the knightly panoply of polished plate armour. Plates, or early in the century pieces of cuir-bouille, or hardened leather, cover the fronts of the lower limbs, and are continued in scales over the feet, and similar plates guard the outside of the arms. Instead of the mail coif there is a basinet or close-fitting helmet, from which the camail, or tippet of mail, depends and covers the shoulders. Circular plates appear at the elbows and shoulders. Instead of the surcoat there is a garment called the cyclas, cut short in front but left long behind, and beneath this a second garment, or haqueton, is seen over the skirt of the hauberk. The spurs have rowels,

THE BRASS OF MARGARETE DE CAMOYS, *c.* 1310
TROTTON, SUSSEX

and the knight, in addition to a sword, has the misericorde or dagger.

It would require too long a space wherein to tell the subsequent changes that took place in armorial fashions, and the no less frequent transformations in male and female attire. The splendid brass of Lord Thomas Camoys, K.G., and his lady, at Trotton, Sussex, shows the style prevalent in the fifteenth century, not only of armour but of female fashion. The knight fought at Agincourt with Henry V, and he wears the Garter of the noble Order of the Knights which was bestowed upon him for his valour on that occasion. This monument recalls the lines of Shakespeare in the play, wherein the king is made to say :—

> A many of our bodies shall, no doubt,
> Find native graves ; upon the which, I trust,
> Shall witness live in brass of this day's work.

The knight is affectionately holding his wife's hand, who wears a kirtle and mantle and a hip-belt. Her mantle is lined with fur and her head-dress is peculiar. She has a jewelled net and side-pads for the hair and a kerchief falling to the neck. Ladies were very fond of nets, which were made of fine goldsmith's work set in jewels. This fashion began about 1350, before which time the hair was plaited and covered by the wimple, a little coquettish curl being sometimes visible. There were various forms of the reticulated head-dress.

Sometimes fashion dictated that the hair should be collected in a bunch on either side of the forehead and then enclosed in a rich caul, the forehead being encircled by a fillet enriched with jewels. Later on bands of hair are spread out more widely ; the horned head-dress follows, and then we have the butterfly head-dress, formed of a light veil extended at the back of the head by wires, the hair being drawn back and enclosed in a net. The pedimental head-dress appears in the sixteenth century, made so as to form an angle over the forehead ; and then we have the Paris head or close-fitting cap with a lappet falling down behind, such as Mary Queen of Scots wore, and in Jacobean times this head-gear was depressed in the centre and the lappet was turned over the head. Hats, too, were often introduced, broad-brimmed, high-crowned, and surrounded by a wreathed kerchief. Such are some of the changes which fashion wrought, and the rest of the costume was transformed by the same agency. With the Paris head was worn the ruff, a skirt extended at the hips by a farthingale and embroidered petticoat, and frills at the wrists.

In our churches it is not unusual, when taking up a brass from the floor in order to fasten it to the wall, so as to preserve it from the tread of inconsiderate feet, to find on the reverse side a portion of another memorial inscribed thereon. Such brasses are called palimpsests. At the Refor-

mation there was a great spoliation of these monuments, which were torn from their matrices, and
sent to the shops of the founders ; and when a new
one was required the tradesman would take from
his stock and engrave on the reverse side the figure
of the individual whose memory he was called
upon to perpetuate. The spoil from the monasteries and chantries, as well as that taken from
parish churches, furnished the makers with abundant material. Mr. Mill Stephenson has been
fortunate enough to discover a large number of
these palimpsests. In our county of Berks there
is a brass to the memory of William Hyde and
his wife, dated 1562. On the reverse side is an
inscription in French recording the laying of the
foundation stone of Bisham Priory by Edward III
in 1336. At St. Lawrence's Church, Reading,
there is a brass to the memory of Walter Barton,
who died in 1538. On the reverse was found
part of the memorial of Sir John Popham, who
was buried at the Charterhouse, London, in 1463.
This house was dissolved in 1536, the monuments
were sold, and Popham's brass made a very nice
plate for Walter Barton. A list of these
palimpsests is given by Mr. Macklin, principally
taken from Mr. Mill Stephenson's notes in the
Transactions of the Monumental Brass Society.
An illustration is given of a palimpsest inscription
to Isabel Copleston, at Yealmpton, Devon, which
is placed on a piece of foreign workmanship show-

ing part of the head of an ecclesiastic, St. James of Compostella, the Blessed Virgin, and the throne of God, who is holding in a sheet the soul of the deceased.

There are various kinds of mediaeval brasses which must be mentioned. The expression of *Memento mori* sentiments was not uncommon. We find them in such representations as the Dance of Death ; in mural paintings wherein skeletons mock the joys of life ; in monumental effigies which often show the figure of the deceased decked in the panoply of war or resplendent in episcopal robes, while beneath it a *cadaver* lurks, reminding the spectator of his inevitable destiny. The same idea is sometimes shown on brasses by figures enveloped in shrouds or represented as skeletons. The common mode is to represent the person partially covered with the garments of the tomb, the face, breast, hands clasped in prayer, and sometimes the lower part of the naked legs and feet being exposed to view ; and occasionally very repulsive details of death are shown. A curious example of this form of memorial is that of William Robert at Digswell, who was formerly auditor of the Bishop of Winchester. The teaching to be derived from such brasses is brought home to those who inspect them by inscriptions such as the following :—

As ye me se in soche degre
So schall ye be a nothir day.

PALIMPSEST INSCRIPTION TO ISABELL COPLESTON, 1580
YEALMPTON, DEVON

Another kind of brass relates to heart burials. When a person died when travelling, owing to the difficulty of conveying the body a long distance, it was entombed at the place where he died, and his heart was conveyed to the church of the village where he had lived, where it was interred, and over the place of its sepulchre a memorial of some kind was erected. This often took the form of a brass upon which is inscribed a heart with scrolls issuing therefrom, with the name and description of its former possessor below. An example is that of the heart burial of Thomas Knyghtley, dated 1516. From the heart proceed three scrolls bearing the Vulgate version of the verse : " I know that my Redeemer liveth and that He shall stand at the last day upon the earth and in my flesh I shall see God my Saviour." Beneath the heart is a figure of Thomas Knyghtley in armour, with an inscription asking you to pray for his soul, and stating that he was the second son of Richard Knyghtley and that he married Joan Burneby, daughter and heir of Thomas Burneby, esquire, and died without issue October 18, 1516. His arms appear on the four corners of the slab. Usually the heart appears without the figure of the deceased. Sometimes a heart is placed between the hands of the person represented on the brass, indicating that he was offering his heart to God in response to the invitation *Sursum corda*.

There are other forms of heart burial. At

Bredon, Worcestershire, there is under a plain arch a stone slab on which is a large raised shield, with two mailed arms springing from beneath it, and with the hands holding a heart. There are traces of blue and green colouring on the shield. There is no record as to whom this monument commemorates, but it is a fair presumption that here was deposited the heart of some distinguished soldier, who died in the Crusades, and whose body was laid to rest in foreign soil.[1]

There is an instance of a heart burial in Chichester Cathedral, where a heart is held by two hands within a trefoil, and the whole is charged upon a shield. There is an inscription, *Ici Gist le Cœur Maud de* . . . At Brabourne Church, Kent, within a rich canopy, is a plain shield, and this is believed to be a heart shrine. At Yaxley, Huntingdonshire, there are two hands holding a heart against the north wall of the south transept. Behind this was a small box which doubtless contained the heart.

In Berkshire at Long Wittenham there is a very curious cross-legged diminutive effigy of a knight on the edge of the piscina in the south transept. This most probably indicates a heart burial, and at Woodford, Northants, in a recess in one of the pillars are the remains of a heart wrapped in coarse cloth, and many other instances of heart

---

[1] Mr. Keyser's article on Bredon Church in the *Journal of the British Archæological Association*, vol. xvii. p. 86.

burial are recorded by Mr. Feasey in an article in the *Antiquary*.[1]

In the account of church plate I pointed out that in early times it was usual to place a chalice in the grave of an ecclesiastic. This custom gave rise to that of engraving chalices on brasses, which are called chalice brasses. Of these there are many examples, which are often useful in determining the shape of these eucharistic vessels in use at particular periods. A wafer inscribed with the sacred monogram is often seen issuing from the chalice. The memorial of William Rickers, 1531, at Bawburgh, Norfolk, shows a good example of chalice brass. The thumbs of the clergyman are represented on the foot of the vessel.

The last period of brass memorials, which flourished in Elizabethan and Jacobean times, produced many examples. The material was then of native production and inferior to that which had been imported. The quantity of brasses is great but the quality inferior, both in engraving as well as substance, to those of the earlier periods. Knights appear in their armour, civilians in their long gowns, and ladies in their ruffs and farthingales and peaked stomachers. A remarkable monument is a bedstead brass, a curious production of Jacobean art, displaying a lady who died in child-bed, the dead infant reposing by her side. The name of the deceased lady, Anne Savage,

[1] *Antiquary*, vol. xxxvi. p. 248.

with particulars of her life and death, is recorded on this memorial.

The figure of the babe reminds us of a particular form of brass whereon chrysom children are portrayed. What is a chrysom ? It is connected evidently with chrism or holy oil, which was used at baptism, and signified a garment with which the infant was clad immediately after the water had been sprinkled on its brow and before the holy oil had been poured. This robe the child wore until the mother was churched, but if the infant passed away during this interval it was called a chrysom child, and was represented on its memorial wrapped in its chrysom robe and swathed in bands, as the little one appears on the monument of Anne Savage.

The inscriptions on brasses of this later period have not improved, and instead of the *Orate pro anima* we find verses that are often mere doggerel. Here is a specimen :—

> Here lyes a modell of frail Man
> A tender infant but a span
> In age or stature here shee must
> Lengthen out both bedded in dust.
> Nine moneths imprison'd in ye wombe
> Eight on Earth's surface free ye tombe
> Must make compleat her Diarie
> So leave her to Æternitie.

This is recorded on a cradle brass in St. George's Chapel, Windsor. Above the inscription is a child lying in a cradle, and the inscription round the border of the slab states that it is the memorial of " Dorothy King lent to her parents John King Doctor of Divinity and Prebend of this chapel and Marie his wife, but speedily required again October 18th 1630."

A curious brass is in Calbourne Church, Isle of Wight, erected to the memory of " the Reverend Religious and Learned Preacher M. Daniel Evance," who was minister during the Commonwealth. Death stands on the right and Time on the left, and " Hanna his mournful relic " fashioned an anagram on his name, the letters of which made " I can deal even," and some rhymes which run :—

> Who is sufficient for this thing
> Wisely to harpe on every string
> Rightly divide the word of truth
> To babes & men to age & youth.
> One of a thousand where's he found
> So learned, pious, wise, & sound
> Earth hath but few there is in heaven
> One who answers I CAN DEAL EVEN.

There is a touching epitaph on another Isle of Wight tomb to the memory of " the religious and virtuous Ladie Elizabeth Legh," who died in 1669. It runs :—

> Sixteene a maid and fiftie years a wyfe,
> Make ye sum totall of my passed life.
> Long thread so finely spun, so fairly ended,
> That few shall match this patterne, fewer mend it.

Brasses form a very interesting subject for study. Impressions or rubbings can easily be taken. You arm yourself with a piece of heelball and sheets of large white paper, which you place on the brass and rub its surface with the heelball. On removing the paper you will find on the reverse a very exact copy of the brass. A little practice is necessary in order to secure a good impression. It is interesting to collect rubbings of all the brasses in a county and to compare them. Perhaps you will find a difficulty in reading the inscriptions, which are often in Latin that is much contracted. Thus the letters M and N are commonly omitted, and a line is placed over the adjoining letter to indicate the omission. The letters a̅i̅a̅ stand for *anima* or " soul " ; leg̅u̅ for *legum* (of laws). The letter R is often left out. ʒ stands for *que* or " and " ; and there are many other contractions, such as Dn̅s̅ for *Dominus* (Lord), Ds̅ for *Deus* (God), Eps̅ for *Episcopus* (Bishop), g̅i̅a̅ for *gratia* (grace), m̅i̅a̅ for *misericordia* (mercy), and many others.

The interpretation of brasses and also of mural paintings and other decorations in churches requires an acquaintance with the emblems and devices of saints. This is in itself an extensive study, and I have written a small book on the subject to enable visitors to churches and picture galleries to discover the identity of a figure from the particular emblem shown in the representation.[1]

[1] *Symbolism of Saints* (Mowbray & Co.).

Thus if you see a figure holding an anchor you know that it represents St. Clement ; one holding a knife is probably St. Bartholomew, by which he was flayed alive. The instrument of the martyrdom of the saints is usually his or her emblem. Thus St. Katherine holds her wheel, St. Apollonia the pincers by which her cruel persecutors extracted her teeth, St. Faith a gridiron and a sword, St. Sebastian an arrow. The symbols of the Blessed Trinity are God the Father, represented as an aged person holding a crucifix, on which the dove, an emblem of the Holy Spirit, is alighting. The symbols of the Apostles are well known, and need not be recorded here.[1]

England may well be proud of the brass memorials of her worthy sons and daughters. Many of them were made during the lifetime of the person represented on the brass. He was, of course, unable to record the date of his death, an omission which his sorrowing relatives failed to supply. This seems to suggest a carelessness and indifference on their part which would not have been pleasing to the deceased. At any rate, we hope they obeyed the injunction, *Orate pro anima*. We have already alluded to the destruction of these brass memorials at the Reformation, when the spoliators tore them up from their slabs " for greedinesse of the brasse." Cromwell's soldiers and commissioners, and wretches like Dowsing in East Anglia, did a vast amount of damage,

---

[1] *English Villages* (Methuen), p. 217. *Symbolism of Saints.*

violating sepulchres and monuments and destroying brasses wholesale. A third cause of the defacement and loss of these valuable memorials has been the gross carelessness, ignorance, and indifference of incumbents and churchwardens, who, during any alterations or restoration of their churches, have allowed them to be sold, destroyed, or appropriated by the builders. I would venture to suggest that brasses should be left on the slabs to which they are attached and not removed and placed upon a wall. This is often done in order to prevent them from being worn by inconsiderate feet ; but the severance of the brass from the slab which covers the remains of the deceased does away with its meaning and significance. It behoves every one who has charge of a church to preserve with the utmost vigilance and care the memorials which fanaticism, greed, and carelessness have failed to destroy.

When the art of making brasses decayed, our ancestors recorded the memory of their relatives by means of what are called ledger-stones, and most churches have some of these large slabs of slate or greystone upon the floor. They usually bear the arms of the family and a full description of the rank and achievements of the person commemorated, with a very fulsome description of his merits and virtues. Most of them belong to the eighteenth century, and in any repairing of the church should be carefully preserved.

CHAPTER XVII

CHOIR STALLS

PROCEEDING onwards, we pass beneath the screen to the chancel, which has chapels or aisles on either hand. These were probably built as chantries in pre-Reformation days by some good squire of the parish, who endowed them, paying for the services of a priest to say Mass daily for the repose of his soul, of the souls of his father and mother, his wife and other relatives. His tomb or brass memorial remains, with the tender inscription *Orate pro anima* . . . happily escaped the destructive hand of such iconoclasts as Dowsing, who roved about Cambridgeshire and East Anglia paying special attention to these inscriptions and destroying them wholesale.

On either side of the choir are the beautifully carved wooden stalls which sometimes, even in small churches, especially when they were connected with some monastery, have rich canopies over them. We are not at present concerned with mighty minsters and cathedrals, where there are such grand examples of stall-work and elaborate canopies, but very many village churches contain wonderful specimens of the woodcarver's art, which was especially bestowed upon these seats in the choir.

There are many churches which are called collegiate, such as Shottesbrooke, in Berkshire, where Sir William Trussell in the reign of Edward I founded a college of Augustinian canons, and others which were cells of some monastery either in England or Normandy, wherein monks served God, daily reciting their seven offices—lauds, prime, terce, sext, nones, vespers, and compline, besides their daily Mass. In these churches the clergy were obliged to stand for a long time and their bodies were weary, so in pity good men devised a means for relieving them during this standing posture. The seats were made to fold, and when raised there was a little under-seat upon which they could partially sit and lean. This has been named a misericord by English antiquaries, following the French *miséricordes*, a better name than misereres, or subsellae, or " nodding-seats." Vergers and parish clerks will tell you that they were designed as traps for somnolent clerics, who when overcome with sleep caused them to fall down with a bang, and brought upon themselves a penance for their inattention to their duties. It need not be said that this popular notion has no foundation.

Besides the misericord and folding-seat each choir stall had an elbow-rest to give additional support to the occupant when standing, which was usually carved, and has a canopy over it richly decorated with carved woodwork. Usually there are two rows of stalls on either side of the chancel, and at the west end, at the back of the screen facing the east return stalls for the head officials, warden and sub-warden, bishop and dean, abbot and prior, or prior and sub-prior.

The carving on the misericords furnishes abundant objects for close study. Mr. Francis Bond and Miss Emma Phipson have written admirable books about them, and both quote the query of St. Bernard of Clairvaux which he addressed to the Abbot of St. Thierry in 1125, and to which I have already referred :—

What mean those ridiculous monstrosities in the courts of cloisters ; those filthy apes, those fierce lions, those monstrous centaurs, those half-men, those spotted tigers, those fighting soldiers, and horn-blowing hunters ; many bodies under one head, or many heads on one body ; here a serpent's tail attached to a quadruped, there a quadruped's head on a fish ; here a beast presenting the foreparts of a horse, and dragging after it the rear of a goat ; there a horned animal with the hind parts of a horse ?

We still wonder with St. Bernard what all these carvings mean, and why subjects so utterly profane and secular and even indecent should have found their way into holy places. They show, indeed, strange figures of animals, subjects taken from Eastern and classical mythology, from the favourite mediaeval natural history books, called bestiaries, from the wondrous tales that travellers told of mermen and mermaids and weird creatures caught at sea ; but that is not all. They show the simple everyday life of ordinary people—the ordinary country occupations of ploughing and sowing, reaping and mowing, the sports and pastimes, the jests and witticisms of not very wise folk. They show what the country people thought of friars and their preaching, of doctors and dentists, of the disputes of unworthy couples and vicious folk, who always met their deserts at the hands of the Devil. Legends of saints, biblical subjects, mediaeval romances and moral lessons, satires on religion and much else are included in the list of subjects treated of by these mediaeval artists on misericords

The subject is so large that it is impossible to treat of it at any length in this book, and the reader is referred to the two books which have been already mentioned, and also to the works of Thomas Wright and various monographs on special series of these carvings. We can only attempt here to show the reader what he may expect to find in the carvings under the seats of the stalls.

First, we will look at the subjects that were taken from the most popular books of the Middle Ages, the bestiaries or books about beasts, derived mainly from Pliny's *Historia Naturalis*. A singular mixture of fable and truth is shown in these early

SCREVETON, NOTTS

WYSALL, NOTTS

MISERICORDS

works on natural history. There were good beasts and bad beasts, and however strange and curious the representation, the artists were always " on the side of the angels," and intended to impart some moral or spiritual lesson, some warning against vice and the results of vicious conduct, some satire on the conduct of worthless friars or monks, or some homely scenes of pastoral industry. The stag is shown as a good beast who treads on serpents and kills them, and so represents the triumph of good over evil, as on the tympanum of the doorway at Parwick, Derbyshire. The serpent always represents evil, but evidently it had some good qualities. There is a curious representation of a snake at Attenborough, which is evidently " a deaf adder," and at his side is the " charmer " blowing an instrument of music ; but the snake refuses to be charmed. So should the Christian man be deaf to the suggestions of evil. The lion is a noble beast, and often appears on misericords. He is fighting and killing a dragon at Manchester Cathedral ; he is stalking warily but fearlessly at Exeter, ever on the watch, telling Christians they too must be strong and vigilant. All these beasts preach useful lessons, if only we can contrive to understand them—the eagle, the elephant, the tiger, beaver, dove, raven, pelican, owl, swallow, whale, panther. All these are represented on the misericords. The fox tells many stories, and is as cunning as the Devil, whom he represents in the quaint teaching of the wood carvings. He has a romance all to himself, wherein he struggles bravely with the wolf, bear, cat, and other animals, and always triumphs over them, until at last he is condemned to death by being hanged ; but even then you may gather from a Bristol misericord that he escaped his doom and obtained a reprieve.

Fabulous animals also appear, and the unicorn is a favourite subject ; one of the fiercest and most uncontrollable of beasts, tame only in the presence of spotless purity. At Stratford-on-Avon and at Chester there is a misericord which shows how he was captured by the craft of a hunter, who took with him as a snare a beautiful virgin. The unicorn at once came and laid its head gently and without fear on the maiden's lap. Then the unsportsmanlike hunter approached and struck a mortal blow with his spear, and the beast lay dead, a victim to man's deceit. This creature is a type of our Lord, and sometimes is shown trampling upon the serpent. Dragons and griffins and terrible wyverns are represented, and many other strange creatures.

When looking at these carvings we find ourselves in many pastoral scenes of rural life. We see three mowers busily engaged at Worcester, and the corn being cut by a man and woman at Ripple, and loaded and thrashed with flails at Lynn. Sheep are being sheared, horses, held by mane and tail, being shod, oxen slaughtered by a butcher, pigs fed by a swineherd and killed and prepared for the salting. We follow the huntsman and hawker to the chase, and see bears baited and wrestlers striving for the mastery, grinning jesters and tumblers.

The chronicle of the months provided many subjects for artistic treatment. Scenes from Bible history and the legends of saints are presented with much skill, and some of these carvings preach wholesome lessons against the sins of drunkenness, immorality, avarice, gambling, while the contrast is shown between the happy home and the wretched one, wherein the scolding wife plays an important part. Moreover, there is always the Devil ready to carry away his victims to the mouth of hell. It has often caused wonder, the presence of certain scenes depicted on these misericords which seem to scoff at religion and religious services. How could the clergy ever permit such satires to be erected? we ask in astonishment. Mr. Francis Bond in his book on *Wood Carvings in English Churches* has been the first to explain this anomaly.

When you see a fox preaching to geese or any such-like extravagance, it is not religion that is being satirized, but preaching. Neither monks nor parish priests liked sermons, and the principal preachers were the friars, who at first were inspired with ardour and zeal, but afterwards lost their spirituality, were hated by the regulars and seculars, and were accused of greediness and avarice. Hence these satirical representations of foxes preaching to geese were only directed against these false teachers, and not against religion itself ; nor did the seculars spare the monks ; but it is a mistaken notion that the Church was being attacked by the artists who carved these misericords.

There are many other subjects which find expression in these curious representations ; but it is impossible in this book to describe them all, and the reader is referred to the works already mentioned for a more complete elucidation of the teaching of the stalls.

In the old chantry chapel on the north side stands an organ. It is a new instrument and was only erected some few years ago in place of a worn-out harmonium, which succeeded the village orchestra and singers who discoursed " sweet music " in the west gallery. Their notion of harmony was somewhat elementary, and their performances of anthems were somewhat trying ; but we sometimes regret the disappearance of the musical instruments and their players. Our church being an important one and connected with a monastery did not lack music, and in pre-Reformation times had a " pair of organs." These were moved in 1506, when the rood-loft was set up, and four years later, according to the parochial accounts, iiij*li*. was paid for a " new peyr of orgaunce." In 1525 another new organ was bought, and in 1533 the great organs were sold to the " ffreres in Oxford " for x*li*. There are sundry entries of expenses for " playing upon the orgayns " and for " syngyng in the quere," and it is noteworthy that these were not all of a monetary kind : 1505—" payed to the clerk for syngyng of the passion on Palm Sunday, in ale i*d*. " ; 1541—" payd for a quart of malmesey for the clerk on Palme-Sunday iiij*d*." When the English Liturgy came into use we find an entry : " Paid Sir William for c'tayne songs that he bought for the church vi*s*." " Paid to S'r Richard a Deane for riding to Windesor for the s'vice in Englishe iiij*s*." ; and " Paid for paper and inke for pricking the songs in English vii*d*."

Before this time it had been protested that " Syngyng and saying of Mass, Matins, or Evensong is but rorying, howling, whistelyng, mummying, conjuryng and jogelyng, and the playing at the organys a foolish vanitye," [1] and the cry for the abolition of organs and " curious singing " grew louder ; so that it was not surprising to find that in Queen Elizabeth's reign organs were sold, and in many places the use of the metrical psalms of Sternhold and Hopkins " prevailed so far as to thrust the Te Deum, Benedictus, Magnificat, and Nunc Dimittis quite out of the Church," and Church music generally stagnated.

[1] *The Seventy-Eight Fautes and Abuses of Religion*, 1536.

Almost two hundred years passed before there was any revival. In 1733 there was only one church in York which possessed an organ. In most of our village churches we now have an organ, and in many a surpliced choir, who if they do not always sing quite perfectly, do their best to render the services with reverence and heartiness.

CHAPTER XVIII

THE SANCTUARY

WE now approach the holiest part of the
church, where the Holy Eucharist has for
centuries been celebrated, and which is
invested with the greatest sanctity. The sanctuary
is usually protected by an altar rail, and probably
a new slight brass one has taken the place of
the older protection. These rails are of post-
Reformation date, and were not required so much
when the lofty screen with its gates guarded the
entrance to the chancel. It is said that rails were
first set up in Elizabethan times to prevent dogs
from entering the sanctuary. The nave was sometimes used for secular purposes and dogs followed
their masters into the church. Mastiffs were sometimes let loose to guard the treasures at night,
and one of the duties of the clerks was to make
the church clean from the " shomeryng of dogs."
Bishop Wren, of Norwich, in 1636, ordered that
the rails should stretch from the north to the south
wall, about one yard in height and " so thick
with pillars that dogs may not get in."

Archbishop Laud, who strove to inculcate greater

reverence for the sanctuary, which Puritan laxity and indifference had diminished, laid great stress upon the introduction of these rails, and many of these Laudian rails exist at the present day. Spiral rails usually date from the time of Queen Anne.

The altar in your church is doubtless a table of wood, but by diligent search you may discover the old stone slab, or *mensa,* which formerly stood there in pre-Reformation times. You will be able to discover it by its five crosses inscribed upon it, one in the centre and the others at the four corners. It has probably been used to pave the floor of the chancel, and frequently has been inverted, so that the crosses are out of sight. Sometimes, however, these stone altars remain, especially in old chantry chapels. I have seen examples in the chapel of Broughton Castle, the home of my friend Lord Saye and Sele (this one has nine crosses), Cookham, Maidstone, Tewkesbury, Grantham, Burford, and in some of our village churches in Berkshire.

In the time of Elizabeth most of the stone altars were removed and a " decent table " substituted. Later on this was brought down into the midst of the chancel and set lengthways, a practice that was in vogue when the rubrics of our present Communion office were framed. Several of these Elizabethan altar tables remain, and can be recognized by the thick, bulbous bosses on the legs and the elaborate carving on these, and on the edges of the table and the lower rails. Jacobean altars are very common. They are low and are not now considered dignified enough for a Communion table, so they have been relegated to the vestry or to some side chapel, and a modern large altar with frontal has taken its place.

Behind the altar is the reredos, sometimes in large churches a great curtain of stone with niches for statues and a carved figure of our Lord on the cross over the altar. In some small country churches there is a screen of stone about six feet from the east wall, as at Warfield, in Berkshire. In many village churches the old reredos has given place to a modern erection.

On the south side of the altar is the piscina, a little bason to receive the water of the ablutions during the celebration of Holy Communion. The origin of the word is a little obscure. In ancient times a piscina was a pond of water for storing fish, and was used in the early Church to denote also the font wherein Christians were born again by water. Later on the name became restricted to the small bason, with a funnel-shaped mouth to a pipe pierced at the bottom of it to receive the liquid poured into it, which then passed away, to the soil either beneath the church or outside its walls. As time went on it was enriched with much carving and sculpture, and became an important feature of the sanctuary. It was seized upon as a valuable architectural adjunct and assigned a special and distinctive treatment in church building. In many churches there were several altars, and each had its piscina. Often the altars have vanished, but the piscina remains to mark their former position.

The simplest and earliest examples are those erected in Norman times, and many of these are known as pillar piscinas, consisting of a Norman shaft, sometimes adorned with mouldings and crowned by a cushion capital containing the bason. Others are set in brackets, as at St. Mary, Tansor, Northants, and at Great Mongeham, Kent. Examples of pillar piscinas may be seen at St. Leonard's, Deal, which is much decorated, and All Saints, Oystermouth, Wales. The next step was to place the bason under a niche, which was decorated with a trefoiled arch and shafts of thirteenth-century style, as at St. Leonard's, Hythe. Then a change was brought about in the ritual of the Mass. It must be remembered that the ablutions were of two kinds, the manual washings of the celebrant and the cleansing of the chalice. The priest washed his hands before the consecration prayer, and at the end of the service after the rinsing of the cup he washed his fingers. Now, Pope Innocent at the beginning of the thirteenth century deemed it unseemly that these manual washings should be done at the same piscina ; so he ordered that there should be two piscinas in each church. This caused an architectural change, and we find in the Early English period twin niches with double basons, as at Farningham, Kent ; St. Mary Magdalen, East Ham ; and St. Mary, Tansor, Northants; or double basons in single niches, as at Eynesford, Kent. The bason nearer the east end is always more highly decorated than the other, as it was reserved for the cleansing of the chalice. It may be pointed out that the instructions of Pope Innocent did not find universal observance, and that single piscinas were constructed in England after his order was promulgated.

Yet another change in ritual ensued. In the fourteenth century it became the usual practice for the celebrant to swallow the ablutions of the chalice. Hence only one bason was needed, and the builders reverted to their former mode of construction, providing only one bason under a single arch. Examples of these are to be seen at St. Mary, Northolt, Middlesex ; Arlington in Sussex, and Great Bookham in Surrey. Variety was obtained by inserting in the niche above the bason a credence shelf for the accommodation of the sacred elements before consecration. A credence table also sometimes is used. These piscinas are important features in the scheme of the embellishment of the sanctuary.

Another important feature are the sedilia, or seats for the clergy. The name is derived from the Latin *sedes*, or seat. It was a common practice to treat the sedilia and piscina as one architectural composition and to embrace them all in one group of mouldings. There are usually three seats—one nearest the east end, which is the highest and sometimes most decorated, for the celebrant, the next one placed a step lower for the deacon, and the third, which is lower still, for the sub-deacon. This arrangement is sometimes modified. The Council of Trent ordered that the celebrant should occupy the middle seat. Mr. Tavener-Perry, in his article on sedilia in *Christian Art*, points out that the stepped arrangement was usual in the early sedilia, as, at first, the assistants were rarely in priests' orders ; but later, when more than one priest was attached to a church, the seats were level. They were also made level when the church was collegiate or was a chapelry belonging to some conventual establishment. Sometimes these seats are quite plain and simple, as in the church of Capel-le-Ferne, Kent, which is only an unadorned recess joined on to the piscina ; in many examples they are adorned with all the wealth of the architectural style that flourished when they were erected. They are set in niches with cusped arches and shafts and carved spandrels, while in great churches and cathedrals they are enriched with tabernacled work, such as that at Exeter erected by Bishop Stapledon, and rising to a height of about fifty feet. We do not expect to find such rich examples in ordinary village churches, but in these there are many extremely beautiful designs, such as the sedilia at Iver and Langley-Marish in Buckinghamshire.

A simple arrangement in small churches was the conversion of the sill of the window on the south side of the chancel into a sedile. Sometimes it takes the form of a single stone chair with elbows, as at Bickley, Oxfordshire, or a series of stone chairs, as at St. Mary, Upchurch, Kent. In modern churches which are denoted " High " the altar is a blaze of lights, and countless candles burn upon it. Our forefathers were content with two only, which seem to have constituted the recognized number of altar lights. This may be proved by the illustrations of mediaeval altars which have come down to us. Very few pre-Reformation candlesticks remain in our churches. They were a convenient form of loot which church-robbers and spoliators carried off with them for the lighting of their houses. But there are several brass, silver-gilt, and copper examples of later date, some of which are remarkably fine.

Our forefathers were not, however, content with the dim religious light representing the gloom that veils the prospect of futurity. The rood was illuminated by lights placed along the beam, and before it stood a lamp or large candle which was always kept burning, and in some instances a circle of lights called a rowel ; and before the days of electric lighting or oil lamps there were candelabra or chandeliers, very graceful objects, usually made of brass, which effectually illuminated the building.

On the north side of the sanctuary is the Easter sepulchre, which is often a tomb-shaped structure of stone, consisting of a flat stone in a recess beneath an arch that is adorned with crockets and cusps and tabernacle-work. What was the object of this elaborate tomb? It was the custom in mediaeval times to enact before the people the scenes of the death and resurrection of our Lord on Good Friday and Easter Day, and in order to impress the sacred truths upon their minds a wooden structure or box was set up on Maundy Thursday, and in this was placed a consecrated wafer to represent the Body of Jesus. This was watched by a quasi-guard, after the manner of our Lord's sepulchre. The books of St. Lawrence, Reading, record :—

Anno 1498. Imprimis payed for Wakying of the Sepulchre, viii*d*.
Anno 1510. It. payed to Walter Barton to the new Sepulchre, iiii*li*. xiii*s*. x*d*.

As this sum of money was a considerable one at that period, the sepulchre must have been an object of great magnificence, and some of these structures that remain bear witness to the same care and cost bestowed upon this feature of the sanctuary. The tomb, when of stone, was ornamented with appropriate carvings of sleeping soldiers by the sepulchre of Christ, the women at the tomb, the angels, the

Risen Saviour. Canopied tombs of the founder of the church were sometimes used as Easter sepulchres. We have seen these curious relics of mediaeval ritual at several places, amongst others at Bosham and Broadwater in Sussex, Stanton Harcourt in Oxfordshire. Some notable examples are described and pictured in *English Church Furniture*.

Some villages contained shrines or receptacles for the body or relics of a saint. Churches so favoured were usually connected with some monastery, but very few of these shrines have escaped the violence of the Reformation period. There are the bases of shrines at St. Albans, Oxford Cathedral, Chester, St. David's Cathedral, and Hereford ; there is the shrine of St. Edward at Westminster, and at the country church at Whitchurch Canonicorum, Dorset, there is the shrine of St. Candida or St. White, who is probably identical with Gwen, a Breton saint who lived in the fifth century. It consists of a stone base with three oval openings, into which pilgrims poured their offerings, supporting a stone coffin containing the bones of the saint. These are placed in a leaden reliquary bearing the inscription—

HIC REQUESCT RELIQÆ SCE WITE.

This shrine stands at the north end of the north transept, which was specially adorned in the thirteenth century to make it worthy of this valuable treasure. In the same county, at Hazelby, is the shrine of St. Wulfram.

Stanford-in-the-Vale, Berkshire, has above the piscina an interesting reliquary which is deemed to be unique. It is in the Decorated style, and is said to have contained a relic of St. Denis, to whom the church is dedicated. There are other reliquaries at Brixworth, Shipley, Folkestone, and Smarden. Some supposed relics of St. Dunstan are preserved at Mayfield, Sussex, consisting of his sword, hammer, anvil, and shovel, with which he is said to have waged war with the devil, according to the rhyme :—

> St. Dunstan, as the story goes,
> Caught old Sathanus by the nose.
> He tugged so hard and made him roar,
> That he was heard three miles and more.

These implements were certainly never used by the saint, as they are fairly modern, except the hammer, which may be mediaeval.

The relics of King Charles the Martyr—the shirt and silk drawers worn by him at his execution, his watch, and the sheet that covered his dead body—were formerly preserved at Ashburnham Church, but have now been removed to the house.

In the north wall of the sanctuaries we often meet with a square or oblong recess which is known as an aumbry or locker, or almery, wherein the sacred vessels, altar linen, and service-books were kept. It was guarded by a strong wooden door, which in many cases has disappeared, but you will probably find the heavy iron hooks remaining on which the hinges worked. Some churches possessed two or three of these receptacles, and a few of them retain their ancient doors or some portion of them. In our Berkshire church of Drayton the aumbry is quite complete. Sometimes above the aumbry is a little stone desk or lectern for the book of the Gospels, the north side of the sanctuary being that on which the Gospel is read, whereas the Epistle is read on the south side. In one church, the name of which I cannot recall, I have seen in a little recess in the north wall a silver casket shaped in the form of a heart. It formerly contained the heart of some parishioner who died abroad and directed that this portion of his anatomy should be preserved in the village church he loved.

Besides aumbries for guarding the treasures there was a great chest, which we shall see when we visit the vestry, and also cupboards, resembling chests but opening in front. My artist friend, Mr. Roe, who illustrated my book on *Vanishing England*, published a work on *Old Oak Furniture*, and therein described several examples of church chests and cupboards. Amongst these he tells of sundry dole cupboards with openwork fronts, wherein were placed every Sunday a certain number of loaves for distribution among the old people of the village. Bread charities are not un-common in our villages, and we still receive the money from such bequests. It was a happy way of securing good congregations on Sunday mornings, and though the people may have come principally to get the loaves, it is hoped that they carried away something else besides. The Charity Commissioners and other reforming bodies, however, do not pay much attention to the wishes of old benefactors, and have diverted these bread charities into other directions.

This mention of doles reminds me of the large boards hanging on the walls of the lowest stage of the tower, recording the bequests of pious benefactors to the parish. These are often quaintly worded and are sometimes difficult to understand, as that at Steventon, Berks, which informs us :—

Two sisters by ancient report gave a yard land one acre of meadow four swathes one Tayler's yeard one Close and a Copps to ye maintenance of ye Causeway of Steventon.

A yard land is easy to understand ; it varies, according to locality, from fifteen to twenty acres. But what are swathes or " tayler's yeard " when applied to land measure?

The floor of the sanctuary has some monumental slabs, or brass memorials of departed worthies, but here have been collected also some of the mediaeval tiles which once paved the floor of the church. Most of these have vanished during

" restorations," but happily a few have been spared and are preserved here. You will observe that this is not their original place, as the designs on them do not fit together, and combinations of four, or nine, or sixteen tiles were required to make up the completed pattern. Some of them, however, show a complete device, and may have been used as borders. The tile-makers were ingenious folk. While the red clay was moist they placed it into a hollow square mould and impressed it with a wooden stamp, filled up the indented device with wet clay, covered the whole surface with a metallic glaze, and then burnt the embryo tile in a kiln. The metallic glaze imparted, after burning, a yellow tinge to the white substance and a beautiful tint to the red ground. Sometimes tiles, mostly of the sixteenth century, are found which lack the white clay and have only the impressed pattern. The earliest date back to the latter part of the twelfth or beginning of the thirteenth century, and bear figures of kings and queens, knights and ecclesiastics, with arms and crests. You can tell the age of a tile by noting the designs impressed upon it and comparing these with the architectural decorations belonging to particular periods. On the thirteenth-century tiles we see distinctly shown the Early English stiff-leaved foliage. The foliage depicted on tiles in the fourteenth and fifteenth centuries displays leaves of oak, and ivy and vine carefully copied from nature. Many Flemish tiles were brought to England in the sixteenth century ; these were glazed and have various colours.

All kinds of subjects are shown on these encaustic tiles. We find the sacred symbols, fish, pelican in her piety, cross, lily, Agnus Dei, cross keys, emblems of the Passion, triangles representing the Blessed Trinity, I.H.C., and M for the Virgin. Heraldic devices are very common, and these are most useful in helping us to determine the connection of noble families and lords of the manor with the parish. Sometimes we find figures of knights in armour, of kings and queens, bishops and abbots, as well as beasts and birds, grotesque figures, and letters and alphabets. In Bredon Church, Worcestershire, there is a large number of old tiles let into the face of the three steps leading up to the altar. The majority are heraldic, showing the Royal Arms of England and France, those of Beauchamp, FitzHarding—a chevron between ten crosses crosslet, Tateshale, and many others. We see also figures of a bird, animals, a trefoil-leaf, and the remains of a series representing the twelve months of the year. These are of the fourteenth century, and were probably made at a famous kiln at Repton, in Derbyshire. In some few instances tiles were used for decorating the surface of the walls.

On the north side of the sanctuary usually stands a special chair that is used by the Bishop of the diocese when he comes to the church for a Confirmation or other ecclesiastical function. It is, probably, not very ancient, and may date from Jacobean times, when so much woodwork was placed in our churches. Cathedrals have their episcopal thrones, and some minsters have ancient stone seats, but our country churches cannot boast of these. Little Dunmow has, however, a fine thirteenth-century chair, which was formerly used at the Flitch of Bacon ceremony, but, happily, is now allowed to rest its ancient timbers in peace.

We have, probably, not exhausted all the treasures which the sanctuary of your church contains, but sufficient have been mentioned to enable you to understand and appreciate its varied contents, and to admire the skill and devotion of our forefathers which they expended upon this hallowed part of their House of God.

CHAPTER XIX

THE VESTRY

A DOOR on the north side of the chancel leads us to the vestry, an important little chamber which contains many treasures. Many village churches had no vestry, which was somewhat rare in mediaeval times. Some vestries exist behind the altar, as at Warfield, Berks ; St. Peter Mancroft, Norwich ; Hawkhurst, Kent ; and Crewkerne, Somerset. I remember officiating in a church near Wallingford, in Berkshire, which lacked this accommodation, and was obliged to robe behind a pillar. There used to be none at the beautiful Norman church at Stewkley, but I believe a vestry has recently been built, which has not improved the architectural appearance of the building. But our typical church has its *vestiarium* in the usual place on the north side of the chancel. There is a very remarkable vestry at Willingham, in Cambridgeshire. It was originally a sacristy or chapel, and was built in the fourteenth century. It has a remarkable high-pitched stone roof, supported on stone rib arches, with open foliated work. The rib arches rest on brackets, with grotesque corbel heads below.[1] Another sacristy, with priest's room over it, is at Bishop Cannings.

The contents of the vestry were more elaborate than the plain surplice, stole, and hood of recent times, though copes and other vestments are finding their way back into the vestry press. However beautifully worked the new ones may be, they cannot rival in interest the few specimens of the ancient art of embroidery that Time has spared.[2]

How rich our country churches were in embroidered vestments and hangings may be gathered from a study of the inventories of quite small villages. Take, for example, the inventory of the church at Hurley, in Berkshire, which was made just before the era of the great plunder. We find that this church had " a cope of white damaske, a cope of red damaske, a cope of blue sattin, a vestment of crimson velvet, embroidered, a red vestment, embroidered, a white vestment

[1] *Churches of Cambridgeshire,* by C. H. Evelyn-White.

[2] The new school of English embroidery, as established at Liverpool, seems to throw some doubt upon this statement. The Lancashire ladies have revived the *Opus Anglicanum,* and splendid work is being done in Anglican sisterhoods, such as Wantage and Clewer. There is one interesting Berkshire village on the downs, North Moreton, a very quiet and lonely hamlet, where the late vicar taught the farmers' daughters and others Church embroidery ; and there is a very fine set of vestments in that little village.

of sattin of Briges (i.e. made at Bruges), a vestment of black sattin of Briges, a vestment of red sattin of Briges, two frontes (frontals) for the high altar of sattin of Briges, another fronte of Dornix (i.e. a rich stuff interwoven with gold and silver, made at Tournay, which was called originally Dorneck, in Flanders), an old fronte of white sattin of Briges, and four alter cloths." This was a fairly good store for a country church. But Hurley was a Priory church, and it might be imagined that on that account it was richer than other village fanes. However, such was not the case ; and if you examine other inventories of church goods, you will find much the same store of embroidered treasure. In other Berkshire villages we find banners of silk, baudekyn (a cloth of gold with figures of embroidered silk upon it), canopies of serge, corporals of white linen or of red velvet sprinkled with gold, with silken cases, dexe cloths for the lectern, font cloths, hearse cloths or palls, Lenten veils for drawing across the sanctuary, pyx cloths, houselling towels, etc.

Some churches would have more numerous and elaborate vestments than others, but in most vestries you would find a white linen alb which resembled the modern surplice, but the sleeves were tight and had embroidery at their ends about the wrists of the wearer ; a chasuble, richly ornamented, circular in shape, with a hole in the centre, covering the shoulders and upper part of the body of the priest and slightly pointed before and behind ; a stole, or long, narrow scarf, enriched with embroidery, similar to those in use at the present day ; an amice, or collar, much ornamented ; and a maniple that was worn hanging over the left arm. All these were Eucharistic vestments ; and besides these there would be the processional vestments, a cassock, surplice, almuce, a collar or tippet, lined with fur, corresponding to the modern hood, and a cope, which is a long garment extending from the neck to the feet made of very rich material. It was worn open in front and was fastened at the top by a brooch. It had richly embroidered edges called orphreys, and is not unknown in the English Church to-day.

Such were some of the contents of the vestry press in former days. What became of all these beautiful, rich, and costly vestments? For the most part they perished at the Reformation, the extreme Reformers deeming that a " comely surplice," or even a black gown, constituted a sufficiently ornate attire for the clergyman. Their value was appreciated by church robbers, as they were ornamented with much precious metal, and the embroidery, which was the work of English artists, was famous throughout Europe and known as *Opus Anglicanum*. Some examples, such as the famous Syon cope, have found their way into museums ; others have been cut up and used as altar frontals, cushions, desk cloths and hangings, and many passed into private hands. Dr. Cox and Mr. Harvey have given a list in their book on *English Church Furniture* of the churches containing relics of pre-Reformation embroidery ; and it is pleasant to find that several quiet country churches still possess specimens of copes and chasubles and fragments of vestments which have survived the pillage.

Curious things are often preserved in vestries. At Frensham Church is a large bowl or cauldron made of copper which was formerly used at " church ales " and other festive parochial gatherings, being part of the furniture of the church house. The churchwardens on these occasions received presents of materials for brewing ale and corn for making bread, and at Tunstall Church, Yorkshire, there is a stone quern for grinding the corn into flour.

The means for inflicting old-time punishments sometimes find a place amongst ecclesiastical curios contained in churches, such as a ducking-stool at Leek, Warwick, and formerly at Leominster, a scold's bridle at Walton-on-Thames and Hampstall, and an iron collar or joug, with a hinge at the back, loops in front for a padlock, and an iron chain fastened to a wall. An example of this occurs at the Priory church of Bridlington, Yorkshire, and it seems to have been a favourite implement of torture in Scotland. It appears to have been used for fastening up persons who disturbed the service. Stocks are still sometimes seen in churchyards, and at Ashby-de-la-Zouch Church there is a finger pillory, which has often been described and illustrated. By such means did the parish punish its refractory members, the implements being kept in the church.

In the sacred building were stored weapons of war, armour, and swords, and at Horncastle there are a number of scythes fastened to long handles which were used by ill-armed peasants at the Pilgrimage of Grace. Funeral helmets still hang over a warrior's tomb, and at Abbots Ann effigies of hands and arms and chaplets in memory of girls who died unmarried. Garlands of roses and white paper gloves also mark these maidens' memories in Derbyshire and Yorkshire.

In the vestry we also find a fine old chest which has seen better days. Much history is connected with it. The synod of Exeter, held in 1287, ordered that chests should be placed in churches for the keeping of the books and vestments ; but there are some specimens earlier than that date. The earliest were cut out of a solid block of timber and bound round with iron and had locks. These are called " dug-outs," of which an interesting example exists at Wimborne, Dorset. Some of them are as old as Saxon times. I have often seen the very interesting chest at Heckfield, in

Hampshire, which is always stated by the late vicar to have been a Crusading chest, into which the parishioners dropped money through a slot for the purpose of carrying out a Crusade. It is considered to be thirteenth-century work, and is made entirely of wood. Another early chest of about the same date is in Brampton Church, Northants, which has some fine iron scrollwork ; and there is also another at Climping, Sussex, which has an arcade of ten arches carved on the front with large rosettes. Fourteenth-century examples exist in many churches, and amongst them we may mention Haconby, Lincolnshire ; Chevington, Suffolk ; and Wath, near Ripon. The carving on the last represents a hunting scene. Some chests have carvings of knights tilting, of St. George fighting the dragon, instruments of the Passion, our Lord on the cross, the Blessed Virgin, and figures of the Apostles and other saints.

For the security of the precious contents strong bands of iron were placed around these chests and ingenious locks added, which had three keys and could only be opened in the presence of the custodians of the church's goods, the rector, and the two churchwardens. Many fine examples exist in our churches, the form of decoration and the character of the ironwork proclaiming their date. There is a remarkable chest at Dersingham, Norfolk, the front of which is decorated by large carvings of the evangelistic symbols with diaper background. It is of fourteenth-century date. These chests have often been treated very badly, in spite of their claims to respect on account of their age and the services they have rendered. One of these I have found being used as a coal-box. A very fine chest used to exist at Tetten-hall. It was fourteen feet long, and was strongly girt about with bands of iron, and was made out of the solid trunk of an oak-tree. It was used for firewood, and many of the books and papers which it contained shared its fate. An old woodcut preserves its memory. If you have an old chest in your church, pray see that the parson and the wardens do not convert it to base uses.

I found such a chest in a country parish in a room that had formerly been the church house and afterwards used as a schoolroom. It was full of old deeds and documents, many of which were of the greatest interest. In these chests were formerly stored the parish registers, which we now keep in an iron safe. I should like to stop and study the pages of these interesting volumes, which contain much information besides " the short and simple annals of the poor." There are the churchwardens' account-books, lists of briefs, and much else that invites attention ; but the day is closing and the light is getting bad, and it will be impossible even to glance through the pages.[1] We have still much to see in our church ere the daylight fades, and have now no time to decipher the difficult writing of these valuable books.

[1] A sketch of the contents of the parish chest is given in my book on *English Villages*, and a very complete volume on the subject was published recently by Dr. Cox in the *Antiquary's Books*.

CHAPTER XX

THE CHURCHYARD

THE evening glow is shedding its calm light upon the churchyard as we emerge from the sacred building. It is called by the tender name " God's acre " and is associated with many sad memories. There " the rude forefathers of the hamlet sleep," and there, too, lie those that are endeared to us by many tender memories. The graves that bear the flowers that are renewed as each Sunday comes round tell of many recent sorrows and bereavements. Marble crosses mingle with the simple grassy mounds ; the bodies of lord and peasant lie there together side by side awaiting the resurrection of the just. God's hallowed acre has much to tell us and conveys to us many a message.

First, we notice the entrance to the churchyard, where stands an old lich-gate, the gate of the dead, or corpse-gate—*lych* is the Saxon word for a dead body—and under its sheltering roof the coffin is placed until the time for the funeral draws near, and the body is borne to the church on its way to its last resting-place. It consists usually of a tiled roof, upon which moss and lichens grow, supported by massive timbers strengthened by struts and braces. Sometimes the sides are enclosed by boards. Occasionally it is quite a large structure, as at Bray, in Berkshire, where the time-serving vicar lived and where the lich-gate has two rooms over it. In the West of England there is occasionally a lich-stone, on which the coffin is placed.

In the churchyard stands a famous yew-tree. The thickness of its trunk shows that it is very aged, and in this calm evening it looks like a sentinel keeping watch over the graves of our forefathers. Wordsworth wrote of one such tree in the North of England :—

> There is a Yew-tree—pride of Lorton Vale,
> Which, to this day, stands single in the midst
> Of its own darkness ; as it stood of yore,
> Not loath to furnish weapons for the bands
> Of Umfraville or Percy ere they marched
> To Scotland's heaths, or those that crossed the sea
> And drew their sounding bows at Agincourt,
> Perhaps at earlier Crecy or Poictiers.
> Of vast circumference and gloom profound,
> This solitary Tree—a living thing
> Produced too slowly ever to decay ;
> Of form and aspect too magnificent
> To be destroyed.

Very ancient are these yews, still full of life, with vigorous shoots and boughs, in spite of their age, which carries our thoughts back to the time of the foundation of the first Saxon church. It was a symbol of immortality and silently preached the truth of the resurrection of the bodies that were laid in the surrounding graves. Indeed, before the Christian missionaries came over our pagan forefathers attached to the yew some religious symbolism ; and when the Christian teachers arrived they made use of this popular sentiment, planted the cross by the side of the yew, and under its shade preached lessons of true immortality, of which the heathen ideals were only corrupt legends and vain dreams.

The branches of the yew were also used instead of palms on Palm Sunday, as Caxton wrote in 1483 when he was discoursing on our Lord's entry into Jerusalem : " Wherefore holy church this day makyth solemn procession in mynd of the Procession that Cryst made this day. But for reason that we have non Olyve that bearith green leaf, algate, therefore we take Ewe isteade of Palme and Olyve, and beren about in processyon, and so is this day called Palm Sunday."

Wordsworth is doubtless correct in stating that the yews were prized and planted in churchyards on account of the wood that they supplied for the making of powerful bows, which did such execution against the French, as recorded by Froissart, and enabled Englishmen to conquer Ireland in 1172. Who shall determine the age of our churchyard yews? There is in Crowhurst churchyard a wonderful specimen which is deemed to be 1,500 years old. In Aubrey's time it had a girth of ten feet. The yew at Fountain Abbey was flourishing so long ago as the year 1128, when the monks encamped beneath its shade before they began to build. We may well prize and venerate these wondrous trees that flourish in our churchyards.

There in the churchyard stands the base of a cross. Its head has been knocked off by Puritan iconoclastic zeal, and some one in later times has placed a square block of stone in its place and fastened a sundial thereto. Some churchyard crosses are very ancient, older than the church itself. When the first missionaries came to England and tried to convert the Saxon villagers to Christianity they used to erect a cross, and consecrate it to mark the place where the people assembled to hear the new preacher and to learn its teaching. In the Life of St. Willibald we read that it was the custom of the Saxon nation, on the estates of some of their nobles and great men, to erect the sign of the Holy Cross, dedicated to God, beautifully and honourably adorned, and exalted on high for the common use of daily prayer. It is recorded that St. Kentigern used to erect a cross in any place where he had converted the people, and where he had sojourned for some time. Very probably the Saxon preacher would make use of the old open-air meeting-place where the pagan villagers used to worship Woden ; and thus the spots used for public worship to-day are in many cases the same which formerly echoed with the songs of Thor and the prayers of pagan Saxons.

The whole story of the crosses of England would require a long time to tell, and I have already written about them in my book on *Vanishing England* and in *English Villages*, describing the various kinds of crosses, market or " cheeping " crosses, wayside crosses, as well as the most remarkable ancient ones at Ruthwell, Whalley, Ilkley, Hexham, St. Andrew's, Bishop Auckland, as well as the churchyard crosses, of which the one before us is an example. The steps of the Calvary are worn not only by time and weather, but by the feet of penitents. Did not Shakespeare write :—

She doth stray about by holy crosses where she kneels and
  prays.

Moreover, it was the rallying-place of the villagers and priest on Palm Sunday, when they made their procession round the churchyard and into the church. When we studied the porch we met this glad throng carrying palm-branches, or, rather, branches of yews, which did duty for the Eastern palms.

Some churchyards bear traces of troublous times, as that at Burford, Oxon, does. On a wall at the west end you can still see the marks of the bullets fired by Cromwell's troopers, when they shot the Levellers who conspired against him. Previous to their execution they were confined in the church, and one of them has left us a memorial of himself by carving his name with his dagger on the lead lining of the font : " ANTHONY SEDLEY PRISNER 1649." The church was the scene of the court-martial that condemned three of the conspirators to death.

And then there are in this churchyard the graves and memorials of bygone worthies of the hamlet. Recently much more attention has been paid to them than formerly was the case. A society has been formed for the copying of the inscriptions on tombstones in churchyards. Time and weather will soon obliterate them, if they are not now quite illegible ; and you would be doing a great service to genealogy and to the memory of many worthy men and women if you would take the trouble to copy the inscriptions that remain ere they entirely fade. Many of the headstones of the eighteenth century in country churchyards are remarkable for their graceful and artistic sculpture, and Mr. George Clinch, Librarain of the Society of Antiquaries, has done good service in skilfully photographing several of these in the neighbourhood of London and reproducing them in his book on *Old English Churches*. In these we see beautifully carved heads of cherubs, festoons of flowers, torches and trumpets and heraldic devices. The names of the sculptors who wrought so well have faded away from human recollection, as those on the stones whose memories they are supposed to perpetuate. I have a photograph of the headstone of a schoolmaster at Beckenham, one John Cade, which shows the implements of his profession—books, ink-bottle and pen, terrestrial globe, set-squares, rule, compasses, plans, musical instruments, and a case of mathematical instruments which looks like a cigarette-case. Mr. John Cade was evidently a very skilful teacher and had very varied accomplishments.

The sadness of death associated with a churchyard is relieved by flashes of humour, conscious and unconscious, revealed in the weird epitaphs that are recorded on gravestones. Many collections of these have been made and printed in books, and it is only possible to record here a few of these delightfully quaint productions of local muses. In my book on the *Parish Clerk* I have printed several epitaphs relating to the holders of that office who seem to have been special objects for the attacks of the scurrilous rhymesters. I will not repeat them here, but perhaps you will like to recall some of the following curious examples of gravestone humour.

The merry epitaph of Dicky Pearce, jester to Lord Suffolk in the eighteenth century, I copied in the beautiful churchyard of Berkeley Church,

Gloucestershire. I believe that it was written by Dean Swift. It runs as follows :—

> Here lies the Earl of Suffolk's Fool
>   Men called him Dicky Pearce ;
> His folly served to make folks laugh
>   When wit and mirth were scarce.
> Poor Dick, alas ! is dead and gone ;
>   What signifies to cry ?
> Dickeys enough are still behind
>   To laugh at by and by.

In the same churchyard there is a monument thus inscribed :—

> Here lyeth Thomas Peirce, whom no man taught,
> Yet he in iron, brass, and silver wrought ;
> He jacks, and clocks, and watches (with art) made
> And mended, too, when other's work did fade.
> Of Berkeley, five times mayor this artist was,
> And yet this mayor, this artist, was but grass.
> When his own watch was down on the last day,
> He that made watches had not made a key
> To wind it up ; but useless it must lie,
> Until he rise again no more to die.
>   Died February 25th, 1665, aged 77.

The watchmaker's trade seems often to have suggested suitable verses for epitaphs. There is a curious one at Bolsover about a certain Thomas Hinde who " was wound up in hope of being taken in hand by his Maker, and being thoroughly cleaned and repaired, and set agoing in the world to come." There is also one at High Wycombe to the memory of John Abdidge, who lived till he was eighty-nine :—

Till, like a clock,
Worn out with repeating time,
The wheels of weary life
At last stood still.

A jesting schoolmaster, who died in 1684, the learned author of a treatise on *English Particles*, ordered the following epitaph to be placed on his tombstone in Colsterworth churchyard :—

Hic jacent Gulielmi Walkeri Particulæ. (Here lie the particles of William Walker.)

An honest innkeeper, one William Pepper, of Stamford, who died in 1785, has the following tomb-verse :—

Tho' hot my name, yet mild my nature,
I bore good will to every creature ;
I brewed fine ale, and sold it too,
And unto each I gave his due.

Thomas Kent, Rector of Donington, Lincolnshire, who died in 1638, must have been a wonderful man, as his epitaph informs us that he "united in one both Chrysostome and Polycarpe," that he was "a Phœnix all eminent, learned, prudent, and pious," and concludes—

Fame hath his praise, ye world his life well spent,
His spirit heaven, his bones this monument.

The epitaph of the third Duke of Ancaster, who died in 1778, informs us that " His Grace's death was occasioned by a lingering Bilious Disorder," and that he " quitted this life with philosophical tranquillity."

A printer named Gedge (d. 1818), at Bury St. Edmunds, has a typographical epitaph which records that—

Like a worn-out character he was returned to the Founder,
Hoping that he will be re-cast in a better and more perfect
    mould.

Vicars and rectors are often responsible for writing epitaphs for their parishioners. Here is one from Dunton churchyard, Buckinghamshire, written by the vicar, Rev. H. Bullen, commemorating an old coachman, named Parker, who drove the coach that ran from London to Aylesbury :—

Parker, farewell ! thy journey now is ended,
Death has the whip-hand, and with dust is blended,
Thy way-bill is examined, and I trust
Thy last account may prove exact and just.
When he who drives the chariot of the day,
Where life is light, whose Word's the living way,
Where travellers, like yourself, of every age,
And every clime, have taken their last stage,
The God of mercy, and the God of love,
Show you the road to Paradise above.

The blacksmith is a familiar figure in every

village community, and the children still love to stand around the door of the forge "and watch the burning sparks that fly like chaff from a thrashing-floor." Here is his epitaph, which is not confined to one churchyard :—

> My sledge and hammer lie reclined,
> My bellows, too, have lost their wind ;
> My fire's extinct, my forge decayed,
> And in the dust my vice is laid.
> My coal is spent, my iron's gone,
> My nails are drove, my work is done ;
> My fire-dried corpse lies here at rest,
> And, smoke-like, soars up to be blest.

The following rhyme adorns the gravestone of a potter and his wife, one John Taylor, of Silkstone, and Hannah, who died in 1815 :—

> Out of the clay they got their daily bread,
> Of clay were also made,
> Returned to clay they now lie dead,
> Where all that's left must shortly go.
> To live without him his wife she tried,
> Found the task hard, fell sick, and died.
> And now in peace their bodies lay,
> Until the dead be called away,
> And moulded into spiritual clay.

At Aliscombe, Devonshire, there is an epitaph in honour of a brickmaker, James Pady, which expresses the hope " that his clay may be re-moulded in a workmanlike manner, far superior to his former perishable materials." Then follows the verse :—

> Keep death and judgment always in your eye,
> Or else the devil off with you will fly,
> And in his kiln with brimstone ever fry :
> If you neglect the narrow road to seek,
> Christ will reject you, like a half-burnt brick.

Punning on gravestones is an amazing example of misplaced humour. It is an ancient practice, and is the foundation of the rebus of mediaeval squire or grave ecclesiastics. Our forefathers loved to play upon words and make sly allusions to the occupation of the deceased. Here is an effusion in honour of a dyer at St. Nicholas's Church, Yarmouth :—

> Here lies a man who first did dye,
> When he was twenty-four,
> And yet he lived to reach the age,
> Of hoary hairs, fourscore.
> And now he's gone, and certain 'tis
> He'll not dye any more.

In honour of a worthy baker at Bristol, one Thomas Turar, who was Master of the Worshipful Company of Bakers and twice churchwarden, some one wrote the following verse in the year 1654 :—

> Like to the baker's oven is the grave,
> Wherein the bodyes of the faithful have
> A setting in, and where they do remain
> In hopes to rise, and to be drawn again ;
> Blessed are they who in the Lord are dead,
> Though set like dough, they shall be drawn like bread.

Many inscriptions bear testimony to the happy relations that formerly existed between masters and servants, when it was not unusual for the latter to remain in the service of one family until their death. At Beckenham there is a memorial of one John King, who lived until he was seventy-five years of age, and was for sixty-one years in the service of the Valentine family :—

From father to son, without ever quitting their service, neglecting his duty, or being disguised in liquor.

A very honourable record truly !

On the outer wall of Stoneleigh Church there is the following curious inscription to one who seems to have been very liberal at another's expense :—

To THE MEMORY OF HUMPHREY HOW,

Porter to the R^t. Honble. The Ld. Leigh.
Obiit 6 Febr. An. D°ni 1688. Ætat 63.

Here Lyes a faithfull Friend unto the Poore,
Who dealt large Alms out of his Lord^{ps} Store.
Weep not Poor People, Tho' the Servant's Dead,
The Lord himselfe will give you Daily Breade.
If Markets rise, Raile Not against their Rates,
The Price is still the same at Stone Leigh Gates.

The voyaging over life's sea and " the haven where we would be " are too obvious comparisons with a mariner's experiences to escape the atten-

tion of the epitaph-makers. Here are two specimens from Selby churchyard :—

> The boisterous main I've travers'd o'er,
>   New seas and lands explored,
> But now at last, I'm anchor'd fast,
>   In peace and silence moor'd.
>
> Oft time in danger have I been
>   Upon the raging main,
> But here in harbour safe at rest,
>   Free from all human pain.

Nor must we forget the gallant Deal boatman
George Phillpot, who died in 1850, and whose
memory is preserved in the following immortal
lines :—

> Full many a life he saved
>   With his undaunted crew;
> He put his trust in Providence,
>   And cared not how it blew.

Musicians have not escaped the attention of these
poetasters. At Holy Trinity Church, Hull, there is
a very laudatory inscription on the monument of
George Lambert, organist of that church, who
died in 1838. I will spare you the record of his
virtues and only mention the concluding rhyme :—

> Tho' like an Organ now in ruins laid,
> Its stops disorder'd, and its frame decay'd,
> This instrument ere long new tun'd shall raise
> To God, its Builder, notes of endless praise.

We should like to have enjoyed the society of
Mr. David Wall, of Ashover, Derbyshire, " whose

superior performance on the bassoon endeared him to an extensive musical acquaintance. His social life closed on the 4th Dec., 1796, in his 57th year."

The following epitaph is well known to all collectors of this curious lore, but it cannot be omitted. It is in memory of a publican at Upton-on-Severn, and runs :—

> Beneath this stone, in hope of Zion,
> Doth lie the landlord of the " Lion,"
> His son keeps on the business still,
> Resign'd unto the heavenly will.

A Folkestone poet, in honouring the memory of Rebecca Rogers, who died in 1688, thus compares the grave to a human habitation in sorry verse :—

> A house she hath, it's made of such good fashion,
> A tenant ne'er shall pay for reparation,
> Nor will her landlord ever raise the rent,
> Or turn her out of doors for non-payment ;
> From chimney money, too, this cell is free,
> To such a house, who would not tenant be ?

The following is well known, but one would hardly expect to find it in the precincts of Winchester Cathedral. The stone was raised to the memory of Thomas Thatcher by his comrades in the Hants Militia in 1764, and records :—

> Here sleeps in peace a Hampshire Grenadier,
> Who caught his death by drinking cold small beer ;
> Soldiers, be wise from his untimely fall,
> And when ye're hot drink strong, or none at all.

U

Time, more charitable than man, obliterated the unpleasing record, but in 1781 the regiment restored it, adding the lines :—

> An honest soldier never is forgot,
> Whether he die by musket or by pot.

Twenty-one years later this stone had vanished, when the regiment again renewed Thatcher's tombstone.

A remarkable specimen of a punning epitaph is the following, that comes from Tawton churchyard, erected in memory of Rose Dart, who died in 1652 :—

> A Rose springing Branch no sooner bloom'd,
> By Death's impartial Dart lyes here entombed.
> Tho' wither'd be the Bud, the Stock relyes
> On Christ, both sure by Faith and Hope to rise.

I will conclude this collection of weird rhymes with the record of an instance of misplaced thrift on the part of one Mary Broomfield, of Macclesfield, who died November 19, 1755, aged eighty. The stone tells :—

> The chief concern of her life for the last twenty years was to order and provide for her funeral. Her greatest pleasure was to think and talk about it. She lived many years on a pension of ninepence a week, and yet she saved £5, which, at her own request, was laid out on her funeral.

Want of space forbids me from giving examples of the fulsome epitaphs that delighted our forefathers and attributed to the deceased every virtue that the ingenious scribe could devise. In contrast to these effusions the simple screed on a tombstone in St. Giles's churchyard, Reading, may be quoted :—

> He was——
> But words are wanting to say what ;
> Say what is just and kind,
> And he was that.

AND so we pass out of God's acre through the deep shadow of the lich-gate ; but ere we go on our way, with memories stored with church-lore and architectural achievement, we turn to view once more the building hallowed by centuries of service paid to the honour and glory of the Most High. The sun is setting in the west, its parting rays shedding a glorious glow over the stately tower and spire and porch and parapet and on the cross in the quiet churchyard. The shadows cast by each projecting portion, by the tall elms and guarding yew, are dark and dense, and contrast with the old grey stones lit up by the last lingering rays of glowing sunlight that impart a golden colouring. Each object we have tried to study stands out in bold relief. It is a picture that one does not easily forget. Its story lives in our memories. It tells of countless generations of obscure and lowly workers who did their best to make their House of God more worthy of Him whom therein they worshipped. They wrought well and worthily, and bequeathed to us this shrine.

Therefore it behoves those of us who are custodians of these sacred buildings to cherish their work, to guard and preserve it. We must let no rude, careless hand dare to treat it lightly or irreverently. Watch it as carefully as the soldiers guarded the sepulchre of Christ. Tamper not with its timbers. Count its stones and keep them as though they were the jewels in a sovereign's crown. Listen not to the seductive voices of the hucksters who offer you with craft and cunning new lamps for old ones. A fool may squander in a week the treasure amassed by centuries of the loving toil of humble and devoted men. In every shire the hand of the " restorer " has fallen with destructive force on our churches, maiming them, injuring and spoiling them. In every shire hundreds of old buildings, upon which Time and decay have wrought hardly, but which might have been saved and preserved, have been swept away in order to be supplanted by some weird construction of " Victorian Gothic." Our heritage has been diminished. Let us cherish the fragments that remain.

In trying to read the story of the building we need much time, attention, and study. It cannot be done in a day or a year. Examine each stone, each yard of timber. See how it grew up to be the " thing of beauty " that it is to-day ! Perhaps your researches may enable you to discover secrets long undreamt of—a hidden Saxon doorway, a lancet long ago bricked up and plastered over, an old Norman font that has been for some years holding a flower-pot in a neighbouring garden, a curious mural painting of St. Christopher beneath some layers of whitewash and plaster. There is no end to the treasures you may find. I have just recovered the ancient door of my church, which the builders carried off when they were busy destroying the older edifice half a century ago. It has been exposed to the weather as a garden ornament some miles away after a long sojourn in the builder's yard. It is pleasant to welcome it back. You will be able to trace the history of the building through the centuries, and appreciate the deep religious faith of our fathers which inspired them to make their Houses of God so fair and beautiful. The art that reared them was not that of kings and nobles or great men. It was the loving skill of the villagers themselves which gave to them this grace and distinction—a skill which sprang from a living faith, a generous love, a whole-hearted sacrifice of time and labour and devotion for the sake of the glory of the Great Architect and the good of their fellow-men. That is the secret of their charm, as we mark each beauty of our village churches, their quiet grace, and sweet perfections. We may admire the grandeur of the great town church or mighty cathedral. Townsmen often built in rivalry, parish against parish, each one striving to outdo the other, to have a spire a few feet higher than their neighbour's, to make the interior a little more ornate. And this spirit of rivalry did not tend to produce the highest art or the true spirit of devotion. The simple villagers knew nought of this, and therefore wrought more worthily. They have bequeathed to us this precious monument of their religious zeal, their piety, their craftsmanship. It is our duty to preserve it and in each generation to imitate their virtues.

Above their red-roofed homes, their busy mart,
  The fruitful cornfield and the daisied sod,
Where they had loved and wrought, and played and wept,
Our sires, with joyous song and grateful heart,
  Lifted this fair thank-offering to God,
Then with His blessing in its shadow slept.

INDEX